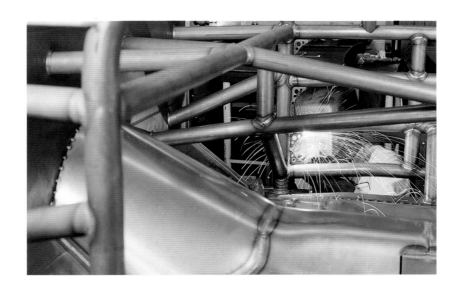

STOCK CAR RACE SHOP

Design and Construction of a NASCAR Stock Car

WILLIAM BURT

MBI Publishing Company

First published in 2001 by MBI Publishing Company, 729 Prospect Avenue, PO Box 1, Osceola, WI 54020-0001 USA

MBI Publishing Company books are also available at discounts in bulk quantity for industrial or sales-promotional use. For details write to Special Sales Manager at Motorbooks International Wholesalers & Distributors, 729 Prospect Avenue, PO Box 1, Osceola, WI 54020-0001 USA.

Burt, William M.
    Stock car race shop : design & construction of a NASCAR stock car / William Burt.
        p. cm.—(Motorbooks ColorTech)
    Includes index.
    ISBN 0-7603-0905-1 (pbk. : alk. paper)
    1. Stock cars (Automobiles)—United States—Design and construction.
2. Automobile repair shops. 3. Workshops. 4. NASCAR (Association)
I. Title. II. Series.

TL236.28 .B8723   2001
629.228—dc21   2001030083

On the front cover, Main image: When a team enters a new season, they like to have six to eight race cars fully assembled before the first race. Although by the end of the season, more will be built and rebuilt.

Upper left: Winston Cup cars are painted pretty much like road cars, but the main differences are the color selection and the number of colors. When a car requires multiple colors, one color is put on the car and allowed to dry. Then it is taped off and the next color is applied. It can be a tricky job for the painter to make a dozen or more cars for a single team look exactly alike.

Upper right: The engine room is the heart of the team's activities. Between races, a NASCAR team rebuilds all of its engines so that when they need to swap one at the track, it is simply a matter of a quick drop-in and the powerplant is already tuned for that particular race.

On the frontispiece: Although a team deals with many facets of racing at their shop, the number one activity is building cars. When it comes to the chassis, the team must measure, cut, bend, and weld many feet of steel tubing. While the tools and materials are relatively low tech, the actual assembly is quite complicated. Every piece must be made to exacting standards if the final product is to be correct. A chassis flaw can mean a handling problem at the track.

On the title page: A modern team may have a stable of a dozen or more cars in various states of completion. This may range from newly built cars that have never been on the track to cars damaged in a previous race and awaiting repairs. Either way it is a constant workload for the team.

On the back cover: Over the years, tighter NASCAR rules and the fact that engine builders have tried almost everything to make the engines run faster have leveled the field a great deal when it comes to engine power. A few teams buy or rent engines, but most have found it advantageous to have an in-house engine program

Edited by John Adams-Graf
Designed by Katie Sonmor
Printed in China

Contents

Introduction and History

Because of both curiosity and lack of money, I have always worked on my own cars, and the types have varied. I skip around manufacturers. I have owned multiple Chevrolets and Fords, a Dodge, a Pontiac, a Buick, and a Jeep (CJ5). I went through a "Japanese phase," owning a Toyota, a Nissan, a Mazda, and a Mitsubishi. My European experience is limited to an old BMW (a 1972 2002 (ugly, but a great car). I currently battle a 1972 Corvette, an old Ford Bronco, and a 1953 Ford 8N tractor. In addition I usually have a disassembled motorcycle or two and at least one old boat. And through it all, only one thing has remained constant. I have always had a terrible place to work. I am currently below shade tree status. (I found a great deal on an old house, but there is no garage or paved driveway, and no big tree that I can get under.) I have worked on gravel, in rain, mud, on apartment building parking lots, and on the side of the road. The only garage that I ever had was one of those tiny deals that didn't allow enough room for the doors to be opened and so was used to store tools and parts. I have been stung by bees putting a starter on the Jeep and attacked by ants while putting stiffer springs in the Corvette. While I was changing the power steering pump on the Bronco, I had a large bird relieve himself on my head. I have had countless unidentifiable bugs crawl anywhere they can, always at the worst possible moment. One morning under the Corvette, I found a black widow spider that sent me running and forced me to perform fumigation unlike any ever performed on a sports car. My neighbors hate me, as it is not uncommon for engines to be pulled in my yard, nor is it uncommon for one to sit for a while before it is taken for machining and building. They have had their Saturday afternoons accented with the gentle scream of the grinder and the harmonious clang of a hammer. More than one hulk of yesteryear's metal waits under faded tarps for its turn for attention. But I do feel some comfort. I know that much of the general home mechanic public is with me. I see

The early days of stock car racing did not have the level of polish of today's events, but they did have the action. In the last 50 years, stock car racing has undergone as much of a change as any sport. What began as a more or less local pursuit by hotshot drivers and slick promoters has now become a coast-to-coast attraction with fans from every walk of life.

One thing that has not changed over the years is the endless discussions of how to get more performance out of each and every piece of the car. Somewhere out there at this very minute, four guys are leaning on a counter staring a camshaft down and wondering how to make it better. Rest assured that 20 years from now they will be doing the same. Compromise is an important part of a team's success. Members must be tolerant of others' ideas to capitalize on the team's collective knowledge.

the evidence on Saturday morning at the parts store, where the grass stains often outnumber the grease stains.

Perhaps it is largely due to my history of poor working conditions that I stand in such awe (and with such blind, raging jealousy) of the modern Winston Cup shops. These shops are the ultimate product of the automotive craftsman's need for tools and space. But it was not always this way. Many of the early stock car racers faced the same problems that I do. They began in their basements, garages, and backyards. Some cars were prepared in service stations, some in chicken houses. The early years of NASCAR was filled with privateers (amateur racers), and many of the first generation of cars were prepared at home. It was a different time. There were no big budgets, and racers scraped around to find what they needed. The fortunate had a large workplace for the cars. The unfortunate were working in sheds, barns, and home garages. It is probable that some of the first "dedicated racing" shops were established because the driver/owner's wife was tired of continually tripping over those six sets of spare springs in the utility room. At this point in the evolution of the sport, the driver/owner still footed the bills. While some cars might have small sponsors for local events (for instance, a restaurant close to the track might work out a one-race deal with a driver), most of the expenses were paid by the driver/owner. And much like today's racing, the prize money was not enough to pay all of the bills. (Drivers' and owners' wives often understood this much more than the drivers and owners themselves.) These circumstances dictated the shops to be simple and cheap.

The early shops usually housed one car, one toolbox, and whatever spare parts a driver could muster up from the local junkyards. Throughout the 1950s and 1960s, drivers usually drove the same car week in and week out. After a short-track race, the car was retuned to run the speedway race the next week. This allowed the drivers to keep the shop simple. But times change. As the sport began to take off in the 1960s and 1970s, the game changed. There were still guys out there running the same

There were no $12 million yearly budgets in the early days of NASCAR, but teams still searched for capabilities. The war to find speed through refining parts began in the early days, and it still rages today. Every year more and more technology is available to the teams for evaluation. Technology can be a great benefactor, but it must be managed or a lot of effort can be wasted chasing ghosts.

car every week, but the more competitive teams began to learn the advantages of having more than one race car. As more companies saw the advertising benefit of sponsoring a NASCAR team on a full-season basis, the funds to have more than one car became available. And the logic that makes two cars better than one also worked to make three better than two. But the same force still drove the decisions. "How much can we afford?" More cars mean more parts, more motors, and more people working on them. And all of this means more space.

Teams then began to buy or build their own shops. At first they were in old garages or any other type building that would suffice. Then teams began to build custom shops. Early shops did not have to house the extreme amounts of equipment that they do today, but every year the competition on the track drove an equally furious competition in the shops to engineer better race cars. Teams began to need space for more machining equipment, diagnostic equipment, and more and more race cars. Teams got bigger, and more employees meant a need for still more room. Cars began to be built for specific types of tracks. Cars run at short tracks could not be competitive on the longer tracks. More cars, more space. Thus the need for a top-notch sponsor became more and more important. When a company sponsors a team, it links its image with the team's. This link is easier to accomplish when the prospective client tours a top-of-the-line facility.

During the late 1980s and 1990s this became more of a necessity. A full-time sponsor became a "must-have" item. The battle for the association with sponsors often became as competitive as the action on the track. Owners, seeing the importance of these relationships, began to do everything they could to better their chances of landing sponsors. When a company links up with a race team their images, to a degree, merge. The image of the team becomes the image of the company. As a result, the team with a great shop (imagewise) will run a better chance of landing a top-line sponsor, not only because of the vast space and equipment, but also because the potential sponsor is impressed.

Unlike most major professional sports, whose homes are relatively evenly dispersed throughout the country, NASCAR's Winston Cup competitors are all pretty much located in or around Cabarrus County, North Carolina. It is a kind place. Most of the local merchants still seem pleased to meet race fan travelers, even after they have been asked for the 10 billionth time where Dale Earnhardt's shop is located. The area pleasantly blends big money and high-paced racing with an Andy Griffith atmosphere. The majority of the teams are located either in Concord, North Carolina, (about 20 miles north of Charlotte) or Mooresville, North Carolina (about 35 miles north of Charlotte in Iredell County).

This centralization of the shops and teams has impacted Winston Cup racing in different ways. It has allowed suppliers of the racing teams to concentrate their effort in one general area. It has also kept the talent pool very much intact. Team members change teams regularly, and because everyone is already so close, they seldom have to uproot the family. This builds friendships that often break team boundaries. It is common to see competing Cup teams helping each other out in a bind. Many of the drivers live close to each other, which also makes for a tighter group. In the past, car owners have attempted to locate in other parts of the country, but it has not been a successful strategy. It is not a wise idea to move too far away from the sport's support infrastructure.

There is one other reason for the opulence of some of the modern shops. Many team owners and sponsors have been very successful in various business ventures. They have deep pockets and can obviously afford all of the necessities. In fact, they can afford the necessities and then some. And they can afford to play a game of trying to outdo each other. Polish to these owners becomes a point of pride. But it's not foolish pride. The better the impression the shop makes, the better the chance of recruiting sponsors (money) and employees (talent), and the truth of the matter is that money and talent win races.

Fans usually only see the pit crew part of a race team in action, but NASCAR teams do much more than what is seen during pit stops. Taking four tires off, putting four tires on, filling the car with fuel, adjusting the chassis, cleaning the air intakes, cleaning the windshield, and giving the driver whatever he needs in 15 or 16 seconds can help win a race, but it is only part of the job. The truth of the matter is that the race is won or lost just as much at the shop as at the track.

The expanded television coverage over the past few years has shown more of the garage action both before

With today's competition, consistently winning requires finding as much horsepower and handling capability as is possible. However, being the best is not the product of one or two big changes, because there is nowhere left to pick up 20 horsepower with one change. Gaining 20 horsepower today will most likely require finding 10 changes that yield 1 horsepower each, and 20 that yield half a horsepower each. This means a lot more thinking, more testing, and, most of all, more hard work. This race is not won at the track; it is won in the shop.

and during the race and also during "happy hour," allowing fans to see more car preparation. Other television programs have begun to show the teams building and working on the race cars at their shops. All of these shows present the competitive side of the sport, but they show little or nothing about the other, equally critical, side of the sport—the business side. Racing has become a complex business proposition, and thus requires the infrastructure and prudent business practices of any business entity. It is a difficult task. Many people who have been very successful in many business ventures fail at managing a successful racing organization.

CHAPTER ONE

Managing a Race Team

The key elements to winning on race day are no secret, and they are easy to spot—a fast car, a competent driver, and a quick, well-tuned pit crew. One or two of the three will not be enough to field a consistently competitive effort. Saying that one of these is more important than the other is like asking which is more important: your brain, your heart, or your lungs. Even if you have the best of one, you won't last long if you don't have the other two. It's the blend that counts. One or two extra seconds during a pit stop may cost track position that may take the best driver in the world 50 laps to make up. Or if the car is not built to the competitive level of the rest of the field, a great driver and crew may never have chance at a win. Managing this blend of talent and technology is the true key to success, and it forms the distinction between the two types of teams—the ones that have a legitimate chance of winning every week and the ones that don't.

There are currently about 45 "show-up-every-week" teams trying to achieve success in Winston Cup racing, but the consistently successful organizations are few. You can count the best on your fingers.

Every year someone begins a new team, and the truth is that few are successful. It has become common to see teams being started and sold in less than a year. The success rate is low and the financial drain on a team without a sponsor is high. Putting together a Winston Cup team begins with the owner (or owners). The first steps are building (or buying) a shop and equipment and hiring the team, which is a multimillion dollar proposition. Usually a team manager or crew chief (or both) will be the first hired. Then, as a group they must assemble an experienced, compatible racing team. Experience is important but compatibility is very important. Teams must mesh. There's an old adage, "Guns don't kill people—people kill people." The racing equivalent is, "Cars don't win races, teams win races." Modern teams now employ anywhere from 20 to 50 or more people. Some multiteam complexes may have even more employees. It is hard work. The hours are long,

Stock car racing began with just that–stock cars. The early races were filled with production cars, most of which had completed their civilian life before being converted to a racecar.

As the sport moved through the late sixties and early seventies the level of modifications changed. Instead of being a production car with a roll cage built in they became a roll cage with a body built around them. These cars kept a good bit of the factory sheet metal but the move away from "stock" was gathering momentum.

Racers like Bobby Allison were not only great drivers but were also responsible for much of the technical advancement of the sport. Allison's career began when the cars were stock and didn't end until the cars were completely hand built. Here Allison replaces the stock "A" arm, or upper control arm with a custom-built lightweight piece.

the season is long, and every week there is one winner and 42 losers. All of this work is hard enough without personalities constantly clashing. A good manager in any business finds ways to bring out an employee's best characteristics while minimizing his or her not-so-good characteristics. Managing a race team is no different. Achieving this (whether it is called synergy, the group dynamic, or any other buzzword) is often more critical than raw experience.

Look at the Larry McReynolds/Dale Earnhardt dream team. It did not work. Why? Dale Earnhardt did not forget how to drive nor did Larry McReynolds forget how to build and set up a race car. There was just never a good mesh. Richard Childress, in a blinding fit of very good managing, swapped the crew chiefs on his two cars. He did something that many managers find difficult to do. He changed things. He moved Larry to the 31 car and got the 3 car another

The "stock" days are over. Cars are now custom built and far surpass production cars in speed, strength and safety. In order to build, prepare and test these cars teams must have a large, well-equipped facility. In order to have a well-equipped facility teams must have a sponsor, which is where the team gets the majority of its working capital. Unless all of the business matters of the team are correctly managed there will be no sponsor, no shop and no cars.

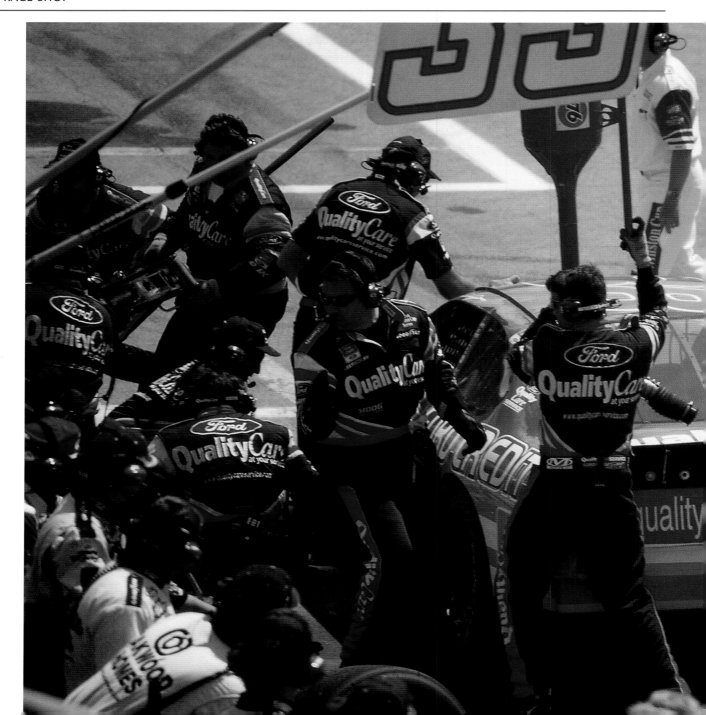

Racing is set apart from all other sports in one respect. A winner can be put out of the event by circumstances well beyond their control. The first place car can easily get put out of the race by a car running twenty laps down, caught up in someone else's problem, ending their day. Its hard to imaging a golfer in thirtieth position breaking Tiger Woods' putter on the back nine, taking him out of the tournament, or a football team having to leave the field and end the game due to catastrophic shoulder pad failure. Even a rain cloud can influence the result of a race, ruining a lead cars effort (but at the same time blessing another car). Because of the large parts that luck and misfortune play in racing team leadership is very important. Championship seasons are a group affair. Modern teams may consist of forty or more people and each must perform to the highest level of their individual occupation for a championship to be possible. There is no doubt that driver talent is the cornerstone of this effort but without the proper support in car building, engine building and pit work the most talented driver in the world won't last long. When wrecks and mechanical failures doom a good team to bad finishes week after week the job or motivation becomes very hard. Most things in life are a result of attitude and racing is no different.

crew chief. It was not long before Earnhardt was winning again, and at the midpoint of the 2000 season was within reach of an eighth championship. Mike Skinner is now running more competitively than ever in the 31 car, bad luck and mechanical failures being the only reason that the car has not had multiple wins. When a manager sees that things are not working, he has to change something, even if it means splitting up one of the best drivers and one of the best crew chiefs that the sport has ever seen.

Winning is not always a matter of being the team with the smartest people or the most money. Winning is usually the product of endless compromise between team members. Ideas are presented, discussed, and then a course of action is decided. This attitude of putting the team's goals ahead of personal ego is what allows team members to communicate and to work together well, and it wins races.

There is no doubt that Dale Earnhardt was one of the best drivers, if not *the* best driver, that has ever climbed behind the wheel of a stock car. Everyone sees this when he is on the track. But what is not seen are all of the decisions that put Dale in a competitive position. Over the last decade, much of this has been because of the managing ability of Richard Childress. Without the latest technology, properly used, and good talent, put in the right positions, Earnhardt did not enjoy the same level of success.

Once the team has been assembled, the managers must have a sound business plan, and Plan One is to get money. In order to race, a team must have a sponsor. This means that getting started can be difficult for new teams, and sometimes continuing to race can be difficult for existing teams. Obtaining full sponsorship can be somewhat like the chicken and the egg. To get a sponsor who will supply the money, a team must be competitive. But to be competitive, a team must have money. It's relatively common to see cars in the race with no sponsorship. This is a gamble an owner must take, betting that his car will run well enough to catch the eye of a potential sponsor. It's an expensive bet. It is relatively common to see a car or two without a sponsor, but it is not common to see them last week to week without landing some financing.

Each team's deal with its sponsor is different. It is safe to say that the more successful the team, the better its relationship with the sponsor. That's not to say that there aren't some teams out there with high budgets and no wins. There are also some deals out there in which the sponsor cannot and does not commit the big bucks to the race team. The plain truth is that they cannot afford the stakes that require a winning effort. But for the reduced price of sponsorship they are content with running well in a few races and possibly missing a few as well.

Winston Cup has recently become the second-most expensive auto racing venue in the world, following only Formula 1. Numbers in the $10, $12, and $15 million-a-year range are now being quoted as the minimum necessary to field a championship effort. While Cup cars do use "yesterday's technology," it is very expensive trying to figure out how to refine more and more speed from these relatively simple race cars. It has been a dramatic change. In the 1970s, a team could compete well on perhaps $200,000. Now that amount won't cover one race.

While money is certainly an important part of the puzzle when attempting to be a contender, it is only part of the puzzle. A fat budget is great, but it does not guarantee success. Felix Sabates recently confirmed this publicly as Chip Ganassi took over his Winston Cup teams. Felix is an incredibly successful businessman. He defines the American dream. He started with little, worked hard, and made millions. He recognized the potential of Winston Cup racing before it was fashionable, and he has had a great impact on the sport. He brought both innovation and polish to the sport. He courted and landed fine sponsors. He works well with his employees and they like him. But his teams did not win. Money will support a good driver, a good crew chief, a competent and well-coordinated team, good management, and a winning desire, but it cannot overcome deficiencies in these areas. As a result, decisions made in managing the team's money are of vast importance, because these decisions decide what resources the team will have and how they are used.

As a rule, once the team is in operation, the primary managers are the owner, the team (or general) manager, and the crew chief. Together they make the decisions that determine the team's destiny. The good ones, while wearing their managing hat, listen to the people they have hired, realizing the brainpower of the entire team is greater than their own. Good managers don't have all the right ideas; good managers make the right decisions.

These managers must make two primary types of decisions—operational and strategic.

Operational decisions concern the day-in-and-day-out running of the team—how many cars the team will build, how many motors, how many parts will be kept in stock. These decisions will both affect and be affected by the team's financial resources. Week to week, the team buys everything from tires to pistons. It must also have a program of testing different ideas, and make the fullest use of limited track test time. Modern Winston Cup racing also demands many hours of testing bodies in the wind tunnel and engines on the dyno. Supplier relationships are also critical and must be managed, partly because dependable racing parts are critical and partly because the supplier can help solve problems that arise as the team puts more and more demands on the race car.

Perhaps personnel decisions are most important, because the team must mesh. Individuals must get along, share ideas, and be highly focused. A team is like a chain only as strong as its weakest link. The entire effort of the team in any race can be ruined because one bolt was not completely tightened by a distracted team member. In any business, managing the people is the hardest part.

Managers must also make strategic decisions that concern the team's long-term direction, although day-to-day operations may affect these decisions. I put salaries in this group because of their importance. People work for money, and Cup teams are as bound by this as any business. Many failed teams spent a ton of money on the best equipment

The sport has undergone great change over the past few decades. Teams now take a very documented, scientific approach to the sport. The checklists taped to the side of Jeff Burton's car illustrate this point. When running for a championship, forgotting the smallest item can cause disaster, and teams now go to great lengths to ensure that no detail is forgotten. Three basic elements define a Cup team's season: mechanical preparation (the crew chiefs responsibility), driver and pit crew skill, and luck. The first two are manageable by the team; the third can be influenced by the team but is really beyond control.

All cars must pass through the room of doom before going on the track. The NASCAR rules level the playing field and ensure safety, and the NASCAR inspectors enforce the rules. When the team is building a car, it must carefully watch the rules from the beginning, because the officials will surely be watching them at the end of the process.

but were cheap with their employees, which meant that most team members were always keeping one eye open for a better job. Salaries are decided by contract or during yearly review, and as a result the strategy used in allocating salaries will have a tremendous effect on the team.

Capital purchases are strategic decisions. This category includes purchases of items such as equipment and buildings. There is a lot of whiz-bang technology out there to sink your money into and you can't buy it all. Good management makes decisions that get the team the biggest bang for the buck. Different teams have different budgets. Most range from the low side of $3 or $4 million to the high side of $12 to $15 million. A team with a lower dollar deal may want to build its own chassis in-house for a competitive edge, but it might stress the budget to the detriment of the rest of the team's program. Many of the lower-budget teams will not spend a tremendous amount of money on a super speedway program. Since super speedway cars are so different from a regular car,

it is a costly engineering proposition to be on top of all of the body and engine differences. As there are only four races a year in this category, a team may opt to just try and qualify, miss the big wreck, and be happy with a 25th-place finish instead of spending a ton of money to get a 10th-place finish.

These decisions are made by the team managers in the offices of the shop. Other offices within the shop house the other critical business functions. The public relations manager is the link between the team and the media, and often the team and the sponsor. Other offices provide the team with the same support functions that any business relies on. Receptionists greet visitors and answer phones. Accounting employees handle accounts payable and receivable, arrange credit, pay employees, and prepare the team's financial statements. Racing teams are businesses and are subject to all of the rules and regulations of any business, including dealing with entities like the Internal Revenue Service and the Occupational Safety and Health Administration (OSHA). These business functions must be performed as correctly as a pit stop for a team to be competitive. Imagine how eager sponsors would be to hook up with a team that has a history of problems managing its money.

Much has to be done to just get the team to the track. Transportation and accommodations must be arranged for team and equipment for all 31 races. This means renting airplanes and vans, reserving hotel rooms, and arranging for parking permits and track credentials. Keep in mind someone at every team is competing for each track's surrounding resources. This isn't so much a problem at tracks like Las Vegas as it is in smaller towns, such as Bristol. The smallest details, such as having medical histories on hand in case of an accident, must be taken care of. The importance of these arrangements cannot be overstated. If a team has logistics problems—like nowhere to sleep—team members' minds might not be 100 percent on racing, and performance could suffer. The smallest error can bite a team. If a sponsor brings some guests to the track and no one brought some free hats to give away, someone will not be happy. As unglamorous as much of this work is, it can be as important as the business of building and servicing the race cars.

THE SHOP ON THE ROAD

Teams spend most of their time in the shop, where they have every tool imaginable, preparing the race cars. When it is time to go to the track, they will take as much of the shop with them as humanly possible. For this they rely on the transporter.

The transporter is a specially built trailer that houses all of the cars and gear when going to the track. Transporters must conform to all of the requirements of any rig on the road. The primary restrictions are in length, 53 feet, and in weight, a maximum of 80,000 pounds. The teams often push the weight limit so close that the driver cannot fill his fuel tanks or he will be too heavy. This may infuriate the truck driver and require more stops on the way, but it gives the team more gear at the track.

The transporter is designed with a center aisle running its length. On each side of the aisle are cabinets and drawers to house everything from complete motors to coffee makers. A lounge is located at the front of the transporter, giving the crew and driver somewhere to get away from the crowd and have private conversations. The race cars are hauled in the top of the transporter in a specially designed "shelf," which is accessed by a lift at the back of the transporter. Quite a load is carried to the track. Two race cars, five or six engines, transmissions, rear gears, many, many suspension components, and at least one replacement for every part on the car is taken to every race. Then there are the tools. Any space in the transporter that is not housing parts or race cars will likely be loaded with tools. They range from wrenches to a computerized shock dynamometer. The center aisle of the transporter is filled during transit with the toolboxes and the pit cart. Because of NASCAR's rules, which keep Winston Cup cars relatively simple (by race car standards), the tools are also simple. Most of the work is done with the same sockets and wrenches that shade tree mechanics work with every weekend.

When teams arrive at the track, the transporter is parked and the team sets up in the garage area. During practice for both qualifying and the race, the garage will be the center of operations. The team may spend 12 hours working on the car at the track. The garage area usually opens at 6 A.M., and on Friday and Saturday team members often stay past dark.

On race day the garage stall is abandoned and the team sets up shop on pit road. A specially built rolling box is the centerpiece of the pit stall. This pit cart houses much of the equipment that the team may need in the pits during the race. It also houses the compressed air for the air guns, used to change tires during pit stops; the timing computer; a television, complete with satellite dish; and a video system, for recording all of the team's pit stops.

The team breaks out another cart on race day, the crash cart. The crash cart is much like the backup car. The team brings it to every race but hopes that it will never have to use it. Crash carts house parts likely to be damaged in light collisions. By having these parts in the pits instead of in the transporter, the time saved may mean a few more points at the end of the race, which could mean the difference in winning a championship. The crash cart houses suspension parts, oil system parts, rear ends, and other "bolt-on" parts that can be changed relatively quickly and are most often damaged in light collisions or have a higher chance of failure.

Even when the team is in the garage or pits, the transporter is still open. Besides carrying gear and cars, the transporter fulfills one other critical function. It is the team's home away from home. The traveling members of the team spend a lot of time on the road. With over 30 points events, the Winston, and testing sessions, these guys may spend well over a third of the year at the track. The one constant through all of it is the transporter. It is a meeting place, a kitchen, and a back porch. Meals are eaten at the back door and deals are made in the front lounge. The transporter becomes very dear to team members. It is the only part of a team member's scenery that does not change on the road.

CHAPTER TWO

Shop Tour: Assembly

While every shop is different, most have a few common design features. One is the main work area, a large, centrally located room where much of the outfitting is done to the cars. This is where the finishing touches are put on newly built cars. It is also where cars that have already been raced are inspected and refreshed.

When a newly constructed race car leaves the chassis and body departments, it is moved to the main area for final assembly. There are many "bolt-on" items that the crews must mount to the bare-bones car. During the construction phase, many of the mounting points for these parts are welded to the chassis, including all suspension and engine mounts. When the car comes to the main room, all of these systems are assembled, and the car is ready to go.

Main Work Area

One of the central fixtures in the main shop floor is the surface template—a level, flat metal surface. This ensures that when assembling and inspecting a car it is completely level (the concrete shop floor may not be). Lifts are also located in the main work area. These allow the team members to quickly access the bottom of the car without having to put the car on jack stands (as they do at the track). Teams will work on more than one car at a time, so they usually have more than one lift in the main work area.

Most of the shop's main work areas have some common features. The ceiling is high, which makes the room look even bigger than it is. Often skylights are cut into the ceiling to provide additional light during daylight hours. The walls of the main shop are usually lined with toolboxes and workbenches and are often decorated much in the same fashion as the race car itself. Around the perimeter of the main room are individual work centers. They may be set up to perform a variety of jobs, ranging from rear gear building to sheet metal fabrication.

continued on page 32

Unless you are part of the team, when you enter a Winston Cup shop you do so through the lobby. The lobby is most often an exhibition of the team's history and success. For visitors' sake, they are often adorned with trophies and cars from the past. The lobby of a Winston Cup shop is a statement. When you walk into this building you walk into excellence.

It really wasn't that long ago that teams bought one car at the beginning of the year with hopes of it lasting the entire season. Not any more. Modern cars have become quite specialized, many being built for a specific type of tracks. Whether it is built for a track that is high banked or flat, a super speedway, or a short track, each car will have small differences that optimize performance for a particular track configuration.

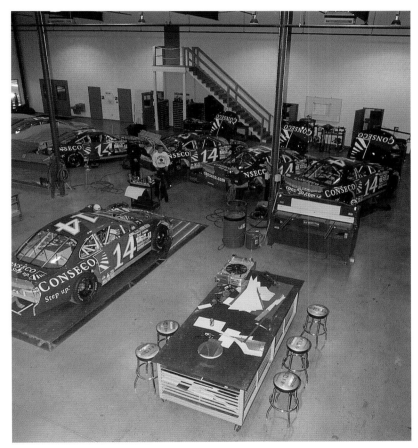

Giving everyone enough room to work is usually not a problem in the spacious main room of the shop. If team members are always in each other's way, time will be lost and they could lose focus, which may mean mistakes. This open arena gives each team member a work area and allows for good communication.

A modern team may have a stable of a dozen or more cars in various states of completion. This may range from newly built cars that have never been on the track to cars damaged in a previous race and awaiting repairs. Either way it is a constant workload for the team. By the time you figure in cars for R&D, cars that must be modified because of rule changes, and cars that have been damaged, and new cars to replace the obsolete ones, the team stays very busy. By the end of the year, the car stable may be depleted and the team will have a busy off-season preparing the next year's fleet.

The primary activity in the main room is the final assembly of new cars and the refurbishing of cars that have been raced. At any one time, many cars in various stages of completion will be here. Work in this area may range from installing suspensions to outfitting interiors.

One of the key elements in the assembly areas is the surface plate. These plates allow the team to place the car on an absolutely flat and level surface. Because the rules are so tight, and the teams build the cars right to the edge of the rules, it is imperative that all measurements on the car be true, eliminating time-consuming delays at the track. Track time is limited during practice, and a team cannot afford to waste time fixing a problem that should never have occurred.

The perimeter of the main room is usually lined with toolboxes and workstations. These workstations are designed for specific tasks, ranging from transmission rebuilds to light fabrication. Most of the special storage devices and fixtures for these work centers are designed and built by the teams. As master fabricators, they take a great deal of pride is building these necessities instead of buying them.

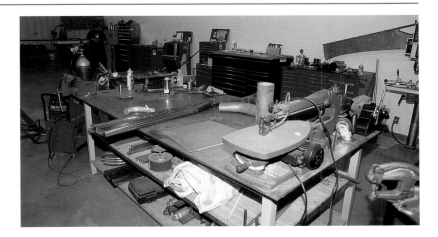

Different teams go about doing the same thing in different ways. Here a hoist is used to place a car on a fixture for final assembly. Other teams simply roll the car onto a surface plate. Either way, these low-tech steel cars are built to the nth degree of precision.

Many teams use lifts to access the bottom of the car. At the track, the team constantly has to jack the car up and put it on jack stands, but in the shop it's much easier to just press a lever and have the car at standing level.

Continued from page 25

Chassis Building Area

Some teams buy their chassis from a chassis supplier. Hopkins, Laughlin, and Hutcherson-Pagan all produce top-quality chassis. Other teams elect to build their chassis in-house, allowing more control over the building process and promoting secrecy. If a team finds an edge, it has a chance of keeping it quiet, at least for a little while.

Steel tubing, the backbone material of a Winston Cup car, is stored on racks in the chassis room. This is how the chassis material arrives at the shop, long and straight. It will require many steps to convert it into the many pieces of the chassis. The chassis room houses a number of types of equipment to accomplish this task.

The most prominent pieces of equipment in the chassis area are the building fixtures or "jigs." The jig is used to hold the pieces of the chassis in place while they are welded together. This allows the team to produce nearly exact chassis time after time. Jigs will be discussed further in Section 2.

Other than the jig, equipment in the chassis room is pretty straightforward. Vertical band saws are

Some teams buy their chassis from a supplier, while others manufacture them in-house. Either way, it is the strength of this steel skeleton that protects the driver and makes Cup cars as strong as they are. Many racing venues have gone to carbon fiber and titanium, but NASCAR has remained true to steel.

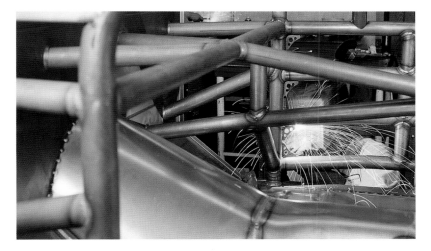

The primary operations in building a chassis are measure, cut, bend, and weld. Many feet of steel tubing will make up the finished chassis. While the tools and materials are relatively low tech, the actual assembly is quite complicated. Every piece must be made to exacting standards if the final product is to be correct. A chassis flaw can mean a handling problem at the track.

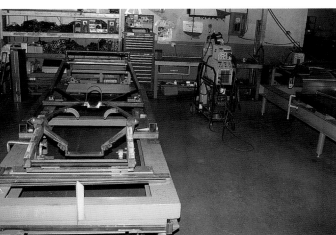

The chassis is built on a fixture, which ensures all of the pieces fit before they are welded together. This large fixture holds the main frame rails, which are the foundation of the chassis. After the frame rails are completed, the rest of the chassis is built up from them.

Subassemblies are made on smaller fixtures and, when complete, welded to the main chassis/frame rail assembly. By using more than one fixture, builders can work on different parts of the chassis at once. This allows them to build a chassis faster and allows a fabricator to concentrate on one area, building experience and gaining even more speed.

used to cut the tubing to size. Once the piece has been cut, it is bent to shape on a hydraulically powered tubing bender. This machine has different inserts, which allow the builder to put many different radiuses in the different pieces. The ends of the individual pieces are shaped so that they will fit tightly before they are welded into place. When it is finally time for the piece to be permanently fitted, it is welded using a wire-fed welder.

Even if a team does not build its own chassis, it is probably capable of repairing them. No team will run a season without damaging some race cars. Sometimes the car is a total write-off, good only for a museum display, but many can be fixed to race again.

Teams not only have to deal with building new chassis, but repairing damaged ones as well. It takes a pretty bad wreck to "total out" a Winston Cup car, as severe damage can be repaired in the chassis shop. This is usually a matter of replacing the front or the rear clip, or possibly both. Once the chassis has been repaired the car will be repainted, reassembled, and put back into the fleet.

Body Fabrication Area

Whether it has been purchased from an outside vendor or built in-house, the completed chassis is delivered to the body shop. It is here that some miraculous automotive handwork takes place. Winston Cup car construction is, in a way, a flashback to the early 1900s when custom coach makers still made bodies by hand. With the exception of the hood, roof, and deck lid, all of which are stock parts modified by the teams, the car's body is completely handmade.

Touring a body assembly room finds little "hi-tech" equipment. There are no computer-controlled machines here; the equipment is much the same sheet metal-forming equipment that has been used by fabricators since the turn of the century.

Shears and saws are used to cut the sheet metal stock into rough shapes. Teams make patterns so the initial sizing can be done quickly.

Rollers, English wheels, and forming presses are then used to put in the complex compound curves into the body panel. While the equipment is low-tech, the skills required by the fabricator are very high. The body is fabricated a piece at a time. When a fabricator gets a piece reasonably

close, he temporarily mounts it to the car to check the fit, takes it off, and makes modifications. The more skilled the fabricator, the fewer times this is done.

A few years back I watched a fabricator for Bobby Allison Motorsports turn a flat sheet of steel into a finished fender for a Thunderbird in a little over an hour. Another fabricator trainee was also working on one. I asked him how long it took him to make one. He replied that the day before he had worked on one for six hours before he ruined it, and it had to be thrown away. And this guy was reasonably skilled. Not only does this show the difficulty in fabricating

bodies, it also shows the investment that a team must make in people. It often means paying an employee for months to train other employees before they can make any real contribution to the team.

When body pieces are complete, they are riveted and welded into place. Once all of the welding is done, grinders are used to smooth the welds. The body is then ready for the final bodywork and painting.

From the beginning to the end of the body fabrication, the templates rule the body. Each team has at least one set of aluminum templates identical to the official

Far left, left:
The body fabrication room closely resembles any good sheet metal shop. The equipment here is much like that of the chassis shop—simple. Shears, saws, rollers, English wheels, and welding equipment are the basic tools. The design of most of these tools has remained pretty much unchanged for decades.

Bodies are assembled with the car in a controlled position. Most teams build the body with the car resting on a surface plate. By putting a suspension in the chassis, the team builds the body with an eye on the height of the car from the beginning. This way, there are no surprises when the car is inspected after completion.

Body fabricators often use large tables when working on individual body pieces. There is a great deal of measuring and refining before a component is riveted and welded to the body. These large spacious work tables may seem like a luxury, but it is a cheap way to make sure that no time is wasted by being in a cramped workspace.

The body provides some protection for the driver, but the roll cage provides the most. As the body comes together, the sheet metal is riveted and welded to hide the chassis from view. The body fabricators work much in the same manner as the great automotive coachbuilders of the early 1900s. Stock car racing keeps alive an art that was mostly lost when mass production took over the automobile industry.

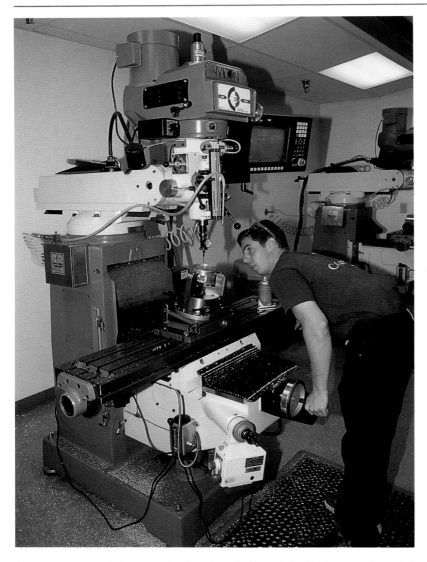

The most common of the conventional machines is the vertical mill. They are often called "Bridgeports" because for years the Bridgeport Company made the best ones (rather like everyone calling any type of tissue a Kleenex). Modern mills feature digital read-outs, some of which can show the tool's location down to 0.0001 inch.

NASCAR templates used at the track. There are templates that run both front to back and side to side at various points of the car. These templates must be placed on pre-determined points on the car, and the body's profile must follow the template within the NASCAR specifications.

Machining Area

If a team is to be successful in today's competitive field, it must be able to refine more and more speed from the same parts. To do this, teams try to constantly better each and every component on the car. Some they cannot change, but many they can. There are two basic ways to do this: by fabricating parts from scratch or by modifying "off the shelf" parts. Both are accomplished by machining.

There are two main categories of machining equipment, conventional machines and CNC (computer numerically controlled) machines. Conventional machining

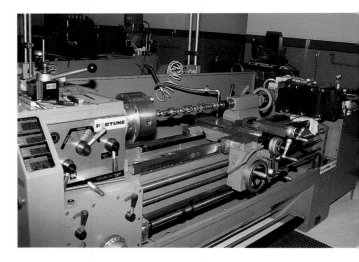

Conventional lathes are used to shape cylindrical parts. These operate in much the same way as a home workshop's wood lathe. Here a conventional lathe is used to turn check the concentricity of the bearing surfaces of a camshaft. While there is a lot of technology out there, often the job can be accomplished using the more simple machines.

Metal is not the only material machined in a Cup shop. Here polyurethane is turned and cut on a lathe to make sway bar bushings. Many, many small parts are hand-produced by the team, usually because cost is lower or quality is higher. Either way the average modern team will keep a few skilled machinists very busy.

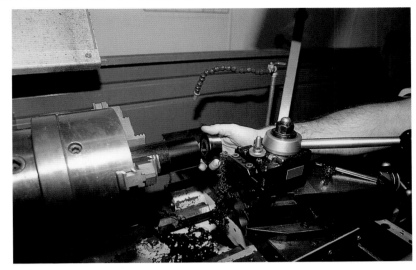

A CNC machining center is an expensive proposition. Purchase price often runs into the hundreds of thousands of dollars, although if it is used properly, it can pay for itself rather quickly. With a computer controlling the tool's movement, parts can be made faster with fewer mistakes.

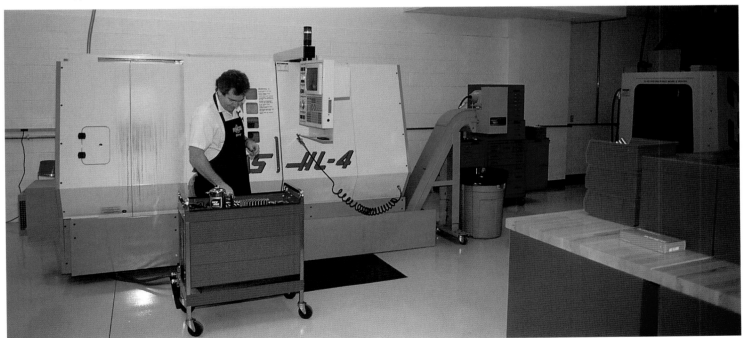

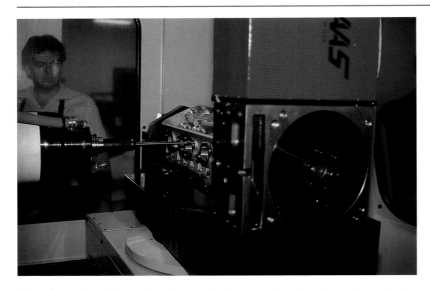

When the machine is in operation, the operator is removed from the action and protected by a sliding door that must be closed before the tool will begin cutting chips. Here the intake ports of a cylinder head are refined. By storing the desired machining commands in a program, and using the same fixture to hold the part, many pieces can be machined to very tight tolerances and be dimensionally alike.

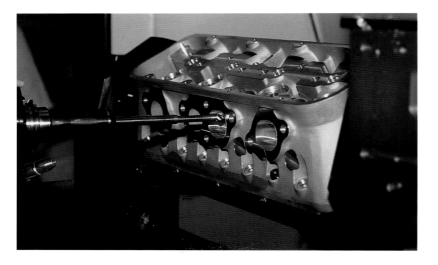

equipment relies on a human operator to control the machine's movements. These machines typically include lathes, mills, drill presses, and grinders.

CNC equipment performs many of the same functions as conventional equipment but offers some big advantages. When operating CNC equipment, the operator programs the desired movements of the machine in its computer. When the programming has been completed, the operator loads the needed machine tools into the machine's "turret." The part that is to be machined is then placed in a fixture that holds the part stable as it is being machined. Once the part is secured in the fixture, the operator begins the machining cycle. At this point, the operator can pretty much stand with his hands in his pockets. The machine automatically reads the program, selects the tool, and makes the desired movements. If the part requires four different size holes, it drills one size, changes drill bits, drills the next size, changes tools and so on, with the operator's hands still in his pockets.

After programming the machine and loading the appropriate tools, the operator's main functions are loading and unloading parts, checking the accuracy of the machining after the part is finished, and making sure that the tools in the machine are in proper working order. After machining, the program is saved and the same machining functions can be performed again later with a minimum of setup time. The primary benefits of CNC equipment are speed, accuracy, and repeatability. Accuracy is better because the machine can place the tool more accurately (and faster) than a human operator. Repeatability is also critical to a Winston Cup team. It ensures that each part is the same and the crew will not

With CNC equipment, the actual machine movements are not determined at the machine. They are decided beforehand on a personal computer. The programmer decides all of the desired movements and sequences of the tools and programs them onto a disc. The information is then downloaded from the disc to the machine and the cutting begins. Again in order for this to work correctly, each part must be loaded into the fixture in exactly the same position. If they are not, the machining pattern will be correct but the location of the machined surfaces will not.

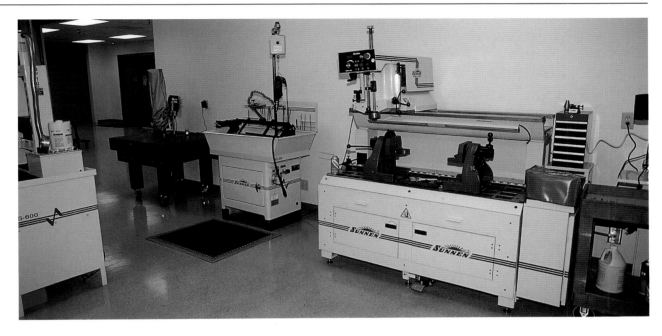

Other engine machining operations are performed on equipment specifically engineered to machine only engine parts. The dedicated machining equipment is located together in a very clean area. The machines will perform tasks such as machining valve seats and valve guides, precision grinding, rod pressing, rod reconditioning, balancing, and honing.

Some engine components are machined with conventional and CNC machines that are built for general, non-automotive related machining applications. Here a cylinder head is being machined on a conventional mill.

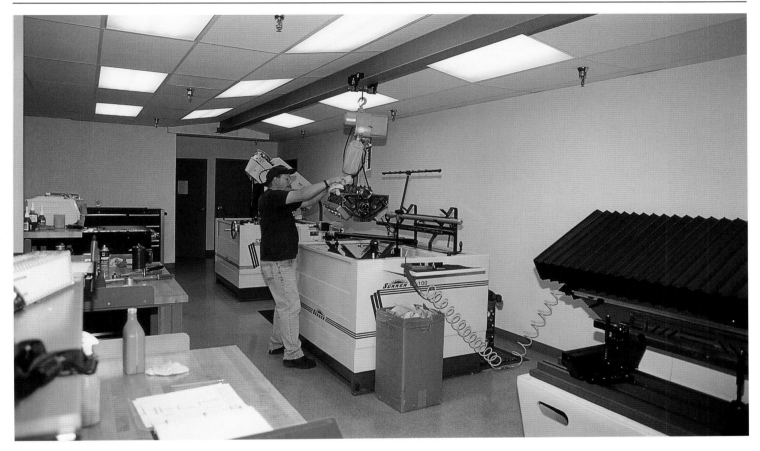

A block is loaded into an align honing machine. Because of the block's shape and the distance the tools must travel, a dedicated piece of equipment was designed to perform just this function. While it can only do one job, it does it very well.

have to deal with parts that do not fit. Even if they do fit they may have subtle differences. If the team does not notice these differences, it is an unknown to overcome at the track.

CNC equipment comes in the form of vertical mills (the tool spins along a vertical axis), horizontal mills (the tool spins along a horizontal axis), and CNC lathes (the part spins along a horizontal axis).

Engine Machining Room

In order to maintain engines and to refine more and more horsepower from them, a good deal of machining must be done to the parts. Dedicated machines are used to accomplish most of these tasks. These machines are designed to machine a specific engine part. There are machines to bore and hone blocks, machines to turn

continued on page 48

A freshly machined block comes into the engine room, as a completed motor gets ready to go to the dyno. A few teams buy or rent engines, but most have found it advantageous to have an in-house engine program. Over the years, tighter rules and the fact that engine builders have tried almost everything have leveled the field a great deal when it comes to engine power.

Left top:

The engine building room is usually the cleanest room in the shop and often more nearly resembles a laboratory than a garage. Once all of the machining is complete, the components are brought to this room to be assembled. It is another area of stock car racing where the tools are relatively simple but the know-how is very complex.

Left bottom:

The need for practice motors, qualifying motors, race motors, and backup motors keeps the engine builders busy. A number of engines will be under construction at any one time.

Continued from page 45

crankshafts, and machines to cut valves in heads. Work areas are set up for different engine parts, ranging from blocks and heads to smaller parts like connecting rods. To get as much horsepower out of the engines as builders do, each component is refined as much as possible. This equipment typically does one thing, and does it well. A proper Winston Cup engine machining room may have upward of 20 different machining centers.

Engine Assembly Area

The horsepower comes together in the engine assembly area. While it is not a large room, it is of critical importance. Once all of the individual engine components have been prepared (machined and inspected), they are brought to the engine assembly room where the engine builders begin their labors. Assembly is "hands-on" work and requires only basic hand-tools. To begin the process, the bare block is bolted to the engine stand. These stands hold the block steady and allow the builder to rotate it and lock it into position, allowing work on the top and bottom of the motor with equal ease.

Blocks and heads are assembled separately, usually by different builders, and are then bolted together. When the engine is complete, it is put into inventory. Cleanliness is indeed next to godliness in the engine room. Contaminants can only hurt an engine, and everything possible is done to ensure they don't get in. This means a clean workbench, clean parts, clean tools, and clean hands.

Here the cylinders of a block are being honed. While the machine tool works, the tool and block are cooled and lubricated with fluid. This prevents heat buildup and allows for much faster cycle times.

Right:
Many engine builders spend Sunday afternoons at home on the couch watching the race, but their contribution is always present. There is no doubt that a few extra horses help a driver, and the engine builders get the credit when it happens. On the down side, if the engine goes up in smoke halfway through the race, it makes for a long Monday. In truth, it is amazing how rarely these 9,000-rpm, flat-tappet-lifter engines fail.

CHAPTER THREE

Fine-Tuning the Machine

Diagnostics

It is not enough just to assemble an engine, a chassis, or a body. In order for the team to be competitive it must know exactly where it stands with each part of the car before it leaves the shop. This is where the team's diagnostic capabilities come into play.

Next to a measuring tape, the oldest and most common piece of diagnostic equipment is the engine dynamometer, or dyno. A dyno measures an engine's torque and horsepower while it is operating. In order to do this, the engine is first mounted on the dyno where connections provide fuel, coolant, and exhaust. The dyno also has a brake, which provides resistance to simulate the drag on an engine as it pulls the race car down the track. Each motor built will go on the dyno. The power output (torque and horsepower) is monitored and recorded at a wide range of rpm. This shows not only how much power is being produced but also when it is being produced in the power band. The dyno allows engine builders to see the effect of

A dyno before and after the engine is mounted. The engine will run on this stand just as it runs in the car. All of the engine's support systems are integrated into the dyno system. Coolant, oil, fuel, and air are all piped to the engine; as a result, its operation closely resembles that of the engine being in the car. The dyno is a very important piece of equipment to the engine builders, enabling them to make changes to the engine and immediately find out their effect. Engines can also be run for extended periods to test longevity and reliability.

The dyno control panel is located in an adjoining room. Here the operator controls the throttle of the engine with a hand lever. The motor does not just freewheel on the stand. When a motor runs at the track it has to pull the car down the track. This is also simulated on the dyno. Resistance is applied to the motor by means of a brake, which is also incorporated into the dyno. The dyno operator can simulate the different demands placed on the engine by adjusting the amount of resistance.

any changes they make and determine the effect on power, from a different camshaft lift and duration to a new exhaust configuration.

One of the newer engine diagnostic devices used by Winston Cup teams is the Spintron. This machine measures minute movements within the valvetrain of the motor as it runs. Actually, the engine does not really run, at least not in the conventional sense. Instead of making the engine turn with fuel and fire, the power is supplied through a large electric motor. This motor turns the engine up to any rpm the engine tester desires. The tester can select a fixed engine speed, like 8,500 rpm, or he can program the Spintron to run a pattern, which mimics a

A relatively new addition to the diagnostic capabilities of the teams is the Spintron. An engine is mounted on the Spintron, but it does not run under its own power. Instead, a large electric motor on the Spintron is used to turn the engine to any rpm range the operator desires. While the engine is turning, lasers are used to measure minute movements of the valvetrain. The information is recorded and charted by means of a computer. One of the first things you notice when observing an engine on the Spintron is the incredible amount of noise an engine makes, even when there is no combustion.

When you get down to it, the power that matters is the power transferred from the rear wheels to the track. Teams can measure this by using a chassis dyno. Engine dynos accurately show how much power the engine produces, but as the power is transferred through the clutch, transmission, driveshaft, and rear end some power is lost. By comparing the engine dyno data (gross horsepower) and the chassis dyno data (net horsepower), this loss can be charted and efforts to reduce it can be evaluated.

The Spintron operator sits at a remote control panel to operate the Spintron much like a dyno. The Spintron can be programmed to simulate the throttle response and run times of the engine at different tracks. A Michigan engine and a Martinsville engine will have different demands placed on the valvetrain, and it is advantageous for engine builders to understand the differences. While all of this technology is helpful, it can become overwhelming. Information is only useful as long as there is enough manpower to evaluate it. If there is not enough, teams can find themselves in the deadly zone of "analysis paralysis."

Shock absorber technology has become more and more important to the setup of the race car. As a result, each team has at least one shock dyno. These measure the compression and rebound of each shock. Since they are relatively small machines, and because shocks are so important to the handling of a race car, the team mounts a shock dyno in the transporter so it can have this capability at the track during races and testing sessions.

particular track. Different tracks place different demands on an engine. At Talladega, the driver never lets off of the throttle as he goes around the track. But at Martinsville, the driver accelerates at the beginning of the straight-away, decelerates at the end, and may feather the engine through the turn. So when developing an engine for Martinsville, the Spintron can be programmed to accelerate and decelerate the engine along the same time pattern the car takes around the track. In fact, an engine can run an entire simulated race for any track, enabling the team to measure an engine while it is fresh, and when it is at the end of its projected life.

Many teams have a chassis dyno. This device measures the horsepower at the wheels, as opposed to at the flywheel. As the power of the motor is transferred to the drive wheels, power is lost through resistance and friction of the transmission and rear end. The chassis dyno provides the most important horsepower data—how much is at the wheel and can be applied to the track.

Engines and chassis are not the only parts on the race car that are measured electrically. The size and location of parts can be measured very accurately using coordinate measuring machines (CMMs). These machines link a measuring probe to a computer and give very accurate dimensional readings. CMMs come in different sizes. Small machines measure smaller parts. This can be anything from a piston to a control arm. By touching different areas of a part with the probe, the exact dimensions of a single part can be measured very accurately to 0.0001 inch. A large CMM, with a long articulating arm, can be

Left:
There are few parts on a Winston Cup car that are not measured a number of times. One of the newer methods of measuring is the coordinate measuring machine (CMM). These machines come in a variety of sizes and link a measuring probe to a computer. The result is a quick, easy, and extremely accurate method of measuring. All the operator has to do is touch the part with the probe and the exact point of contact is recorded. As the operator touches more critical measuring points, the computer calculates distances and angles between the selected points. Parts that may take hours to inspect with calipers and gauges can be measured more accurately, in minutes, using a CMM.

The cars are prepared for painting in an area outside of the paint booth. Because of the large amounts of dust generated by all of the sanding, hoods and vents suck as much of it out of the shop as is possible.

Primarily due to government regulations aimed at keeping the environment clean, teams use paint booths that contain all of the overspray that does not reach the car. The air entering the booth is filtered to ensure that only clean air comes in, eliminating dust particles and other possible contaminates. The air being pulled from the booth is filtered to remove any paint or chemical contaminates before it is released back into the environment.

Winston Cup cars are painted pretty much like road cars, the main differences being the color selection and the number of colors. When a car requires multiple colors, one color is put on the car and allowed to dry. Then it is taped off and the next color is applied. It can be a tricky job for the painter to make a dozen or more cars look exactly alike.

used to measure an entire car—body or suspension or both. These machines are faster and more accurate than old measuring methods.

Some smaller components of the car require their own diagnostic systems. Shock absorbers are a prime example. Shocks have become very important to the handling of the race car. As a result, teams use a "shock dyno" to measure each shock's performance. They measure and record the resistance in both the compression and rebound stroke of the shock absorber.

Paint Area

The last step in the body assembly is painting. First, any seams or other irregularities are smoothed out of the body. The fabricators say that there is little smoothing to be done. The painters often argue this point. There can be no doubt that over the last decade the body assembly has gotten more accurate. One body builder observed this team progress as the amount of body filler required to finish a car has dropped from almost 2 gallons to 2 quarts over the past few years. After the filler has been applied, the cars are primered. Cars are often taken to the track and tested in a primered state and are not painted until the car is ready to head to the race.

Just like any other paint shop, the teams must comply with all local, state, and federal regulations. The primary concerns are the painter's safety and environmental safety. Modern paint booths have filter systems, which catch paint that stays in the air and not on the car. Painters also wear suits and masks to limit their exposure.

The paint booth is also quite clean. Ventilation systems and filters keep dust and other airborne objects out of the paint. Computers control modern paint booths. This allows the painter to program both the ventilation and temperature in the booth. As a result, the paint jobs on a Winston Cup car are as slick as any on the road.

Dirty Room

Every shop will have at least one "dirty room." One of the goals of every shop manager is to keep the shop as clean as possible. Concentrating the dirtier jobs in one area helps keep the rest of the shop clean. Dirty rooms are used for cleaning everything from an entire race car to individual parts. Race cars can get quite dirty during

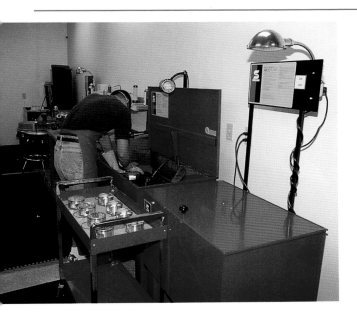

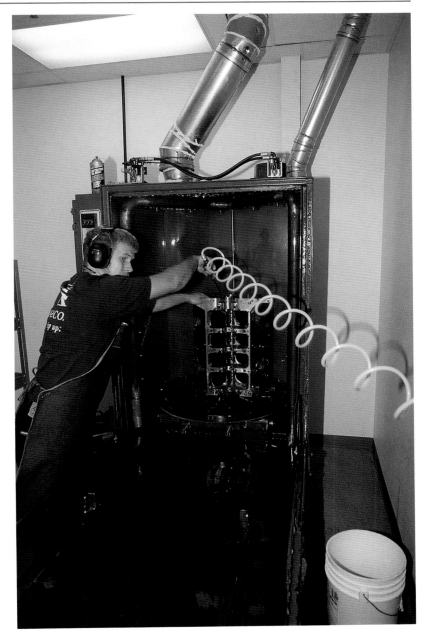

Left, above and right:
A great deal of effort goes into keeping the shops as clean as possible. One contributing factor to this effort is isolating as many inherently dirty jobs as possible in an attempt to never let the dirt into the shop. This primarily consists of cleaning operations and hand-grinding. Cleaning may range from chemically washing parts (above) to using blast equipment (right). Grinding stations are set up on a bench in an isolated areas, some having a vacuum hood to help contain dust (left).

a race. Dust, oil film, and grime will always be there, and if the car takes an "off track" adventure, dirt will get in every nook and cranny. Cars can also get a good bit of rubber built up on them. Racing tires are much softer that street tires, the main reason that they handle so much better, and the reason they do not last very long. During a race, the abrasive track grinds small pieces of this hot soft rubber off of the tire. Much of this rubber goes onto the track, but a good bit of it gets caked up into the fender wells and under the car. The dirty room

A modern Winston Cup shop will house a large inventory of parts. In the storage room, shelf after shelf of parts are neatly arranged. This shelf houses shocks, springs, cylinder heads, radiators, and hoses, and the list goes on. All of the parts in the storage area have one thing in common—they are expensive.

is usually the place where a lucky team member gets the glamorous job of scraping the rubber off.

Dirty rooms usually have a pressure washer, steam cleaner, and a chemical parts washing station. Often the shop's grinders are located in the dirty room to keep the grinding dust from spreading through out the entire shop.

Storage Area

It takes a lot of stuff to keep a Winston Cup team afloat. A whole lot of stuff. While the concentration of suppliers around the shops is helpful, teams must still keep a large inventory on hand. Time cannot be wasted running to the store when the team is trying to get a car ready to go to the track. As in any storage facility, neatness and organization are mandatory. The time a team member can save looking for a part can be spent working on the race car. Shelf after shelf is filled with every part necessary to build and maintain a fleet of race cars. Some parts, because of their ungainly shapes, must be secured in custom storage devices while others fill up shelf after shelf.

When building a Winston Cup car, teams use three types of parts—stock, aftermarket, and handmade. The stock pieces are few and far between. Parts of the body, roof, hood, and rear deck lid are factory "skins." The skins are the outer sheet metal without the factory backing structures and reinforcements. And that's about it for the factory parts (*stock* cars, huh?). Many, many parts of the car are from the aftermarket. These are parts specifically engineered for racing by independent companies that are usually not affiliated with an original equipment manufacturer (OEM). These parts are usually stronger than their stock counterparts, and they are often lighter. This is accomplished by using more advanced designs and strong lightweight materials, primarily aluminum. Only aftermarket parts that conform to NASCAR's rules may be used. Aftermarket parts range from pistons to tachometers. Teams may also put their own custom touches or modifications on aftermarket parts. The third category of parts, handmade, includes all of the parts designed, engineered, and built by the teams. The biggest of these is the frame/roll cage and the body, although many other bits of the car, from brackets to suspension parts, are built from scratch by the teams.

NASCAR watches these modifications closely. Any modifications from the traditional design must be submitted to the NASCAR series director (in blueprint form) at least 60 days before the car is to compete. If the new design is approved, the competitor must submit the completed frame and chassis for inspection at least 30 days before the car is to compete on the track. Even if NASCAR approves the blueprint, it does not necessarily mean that the completed chassis will be accepted.

Most shops have a full-time parts manager to keep an eye on a very valuable inventory. All parts must be checked in and out of storage, so cost can be tracked and replacements ordered.

The parts warehouse is an area where proper business practices benefit a team. Parts must be properly checked out if a replacement is to be bought. They must properly be checked in so that inventory can be tracked. The total inventory can be of great value and, like any financial commitment, it must be properly managed. On most teams this is a full-time job. Having one employee maintain this area will give the team benefits that far outweigh the cost of his or her salary.

Outside

The outside of the shop is usually decorative in the front and functional in the rear. The front of Winston Cup shops varies. Most are nicely landscaped. Were it not for the signs and the sound of an engine screaming on the

Out back there is usually a place to store some gear. Here the team's tires and wheels, a bulky commodity, are put under a shed to provide more room inside the shop.

dyno, a pedestrian might mistake the shop for any prosperous service company. Other shops have fronts that more resemble a country club or a concert hall. Whether it is acres of manicured lawn, lakes with fountains, or landscaping comparable to Augusta National, they incorporate features aimed solely at showmanship. As discussed earlier, indirect benefits, such as pride and impressing sponsors, are associated with such opulence.

The rear of the shop has a paved area large enough for the transporter to maneuver. A covered area is sometimes built for the transporter to be stored during the week and during the off-season. Often one or more buildings are located in the rear of the shop for storage. Racers are human too. Like the rest of us, they tend to keep some things that they don't really need but don't want to get rid of. In an effort to keep this stuff from getting in the way of the team's main effort, they often store it "out back."

The pit crew's practice area is usually located behind the shop. It consists of little more than a replica section of the pit wall. It may be simple, but it is of vast importance. With the cars as equal as they are, track position has become more and more critical. Even if a driver has the fastest car on the track, a bad pit stop can move him from 1st to 20th. By the time the driver works his way through all of the traffic (if he can, and if he can do it without getting caught up in an accident), he will probably have used up his tires and will no longer be the fastest car. Likewise, there is no better way for a driver to pass than in the pits. With a great pit stop, a driver can go from 5th to 1st, and he will not use up tires or bang any fenders doing it.

Personnel Areas

As racing became more business than hobby, owners began to recognize the importance of both mental and physical fitness. As a result, the shops became a tool to improve both. As discussed earlier, the professional and polished finish of the shops makes an impact on the spirit. Let's face it—if you work in a dark, dirty, and cramped workplace, you are much more likely to have a dark, dirty, and cramped attitude. The reverse is also true. If you have a well-lighted, clean, and spacious work area, it is much easier to keep a good attitude. So the extra expense of "polishing" a race shop is not entirely ego. (It's partly ego, but not completely.) If it makes for better attitude, then it is worth it.

Many shops have a break room in-house. It gives team members place to relax and unwind during breaks and lunch. Another "in-house" necessity is a weight room. Physical training has become a necessity for many team members. Although some engine builders out there would fall to pieces if they had to run a mile, the active crew can greatly increase its chance of success by being as fit as possible. Obviously, the pit crew needs to be in the best possible shape. Strength, speed, and dexterity will pay off in

This is one of the simplest tools at any shop, but is one of the most important—a concrete block wall. Every day the pit crew gravitates to this little piece of rock to practice pit stops. Practice makes perfect, and it also helps keep everyone in shape. By watching the pit stop speeds on Sunday you can tell which team spends the most time at the wall.

shorter pit times. But all of the team can benefit from being in shape. Running around the garage all weekend constantly working on the race car is physically demanding. The day starts early at the track. Team members are usually lined up at the garage gate at 5:45 A.M. This usually means getting out of bed by 4 or 4:30 a.m. Once at the track, most of the "glamorous" racing work consists of pushing the car, jacking up the car, and changing parts on the car. Some of the less-glamorous work is unloading the transporter, and pushing toolboxes, pit carts, and crash carts around the garage area. Team members are constantly going from the transporter to the garage to the pits. They walk on concrete all day and they seldom get the chance to sit down. They usually leave the track at 6 or 7 P.M. It's a 12-hour workday before they leave to go back to the hotel. The better physical shape team members are in, the better their chances of living through it.

CHAPTER FOUR

Building a Chassis

Richard Petty once remarked that the car builder's effort, building a Winston Cup race car from scratch, is a contribution to art. I agree. Their expression of excellence touches the soul of a shade tree mechanic or a fabricator just as a Picasso touches an art critic. Modern Winston Cup cars are built much more along the line of handcraft than any of their production counterparts. Large forges and robotic welders spit out cars built for the road. The primary human contribution is assembling components, and subassemblies, which are too difficult (meaning costly) to automate. Modern "stock cars" are hand-assembled at every stage, and many components are hand-built. From roll bars to fenders, many pieces of the car begin as stock metal products (steel tubing and steel sheet metal) that can be bought in from any steel supplier. The result is that the Winston Cup cars racing today look somewhat like the production cars they are named after, but they have very little else in common.

Engineering and building a Winston Cup car is something of a paradox. It can be said that Winston Cup cars are on the cutting edge of yesterday's technology. With a steel chassis, a steel body, pushrod V-8 power, and a solid rear axle, Cup cars are not on the cutting edge of modern automotive technology. Teams do not rely on huge engineering breakthroughs in materials and systems to increase horsepower and handling. Rather, the teams must keep refining the existing technology by using experience, trial-and-error testing, and an open mind. That's not to say that fielding a successful Winston Cup race car is not as difficult as fielding an Indy, Cart, or Formula One car. It's my opinion that it is—well, maybe not as difficult as F1, but that's only because nobody seems to speak the same language. NASCAR has just chosen a different way of going at it. It's NASCAR's way, and it works. Nonetheless, calling a Winston Cup car a "stock" car is about like calling a Saturn V rocket a "stock" bottle rocket. From a distance (a good distance) with stock paint, no stickers, regular wheels and tires, and no spoiler (and if you squint your eyes some) they kind of look stock. You may wonder why I take the time to

Today there are few pieces of a Cup car that can be considered "stock." Just about every piece of the car is either hand built by the team or bought from an aftermarket supplier who make dedicated racing components.

point out something so obvious. A few years back I was watching the race on Sunday afternoon and there was a rain delay. After a while, in a search for something to talk about, the network opened up the phone lines and allowed race fans watching at home the opportunity to ask the commentators some questions. The questions were interesting. Some were about wedge and track bars and such, but I remember one guy asking if the race cars were front-wheel drive like the stock version. Not long thereafter, another asked if they ran four- or six-cylinder engines. Perhaps this tag of "stock" has some who only watch on television a bit confused about the true configuration of the cars.

NASCAR began its first full, sanctioned season in 1949. During the 1950s and 1960s the race cars that were run on Sunday were all modified production cars. During this period, the racers ran the same cars that could be bought by the consumer at any dealership. As time went on, they were modified more and more with better roll bars, hotter engines, and a suspension that became more and more tuned for racing. But it changed in the late 1960s and early 1970s. Production cars would be left at the dealership and custom-built race cars began to take over the circuit.

Now all of the cars competing on the Winston Cup circuit are custom built. Many different teams and suppliers are building cars, but they all must conform to NASCAR specifications, which eliminate many of today's exotic materials and designs for everything except the safety systems of the car. Concepts and systems seen in other racing venues, such as turbochargers, overhead-cam engine configurations, advanced aerodynamics, in-car computer telemetry, and extensive use of exotic materials—carbon fiber, titanium, etc.—are not allowed in Winston Cup racing. Again, this forces the teams to rely on the better engineering of old technology and refinement of the race setup. Winston Cup team members make many small changes to the cars and engines that may not seem too much individually. When these small changes are added

up, however, they can make the difference between winning and being an also-ran.

As a result, NASCAR's limiting rules provide for safe and very competitive racing on the track, and they set the stage for another competition—the constant race within the shops. By discussion and testing, whether it is a practice session at Martinsville or a three-day wind tunnel test, the teams are constantly learning more and more about the forces that race cars encounter and the components on the cars that counter those forces. By constantly "tweaking" and fine-tuning each component and system on the race car, the teams can achieve greater speeds every year. Many times in the past, the rules have been changed to slow the cars down. A good example of this is Daytona and Talladega. After a few accidents (mainly Bobby Allison getting into the fence at Talladega), NASCAR began mandating the use of carburetor restrictor plates to slow the cars down. This forced the engineers to look for more speed by refining aerodynamics, handling, and the engine itself. It pushed the teams to search for any change that would give that small but important advantage on the track. As a result the speeds went back up, and the holes in the restrictor plates got even smaller.

This competitive racing is a benefit for the fan, but it is a double-edged sword, and the owners feel the other side, the cost side. The search for speed is expensive. Many still quote the adage "Speed costs, now how fast do you want to go?" It was not long ago that a team could run a whole year for the current cost of one race. Recently, when discussing the current price of Winston Cup shock absorbers (around $2,800 a set), Buddy Baker remarked that he paid $2,500 for one of his first race cars and raced it all year.

Building the Chassis

A Winston Cup car's chassis, which includes the frame and roll cage, is born on the jig. The jig is a large fixture on which the frames and roll cages are built. These fixtures give the car builders two things that are of critical importance when building any mechanical device—accuracy and

The modern Winston Cup chassis is probably the most graphic example of how much the sport has changed over the last 50 years. While modern chassis provide for better handling race cars, the greatest benefit has been in the area of driver safety. Without all of this steel surrounding them, many drivers could not walk away from many of the high-speed accidents that unfortunately happen every year.

repeatability. Accuracy is obviously important. The finished product must meet the specifications of the team, and it must meet the specifications of NASCAR. If the final product is to meet these specifications, every piece must go together correctly. The pieces must be the right size, and all of the welded connections must be in the right place. By clamping them into the fixture, any problem can be identified and a mistake will be caught before it is built into the car.

Repeatability is important, because the team must have control over the chassis if its track notes are to mean anything. Crew chiefs keep extensive notes of all setups that have been run at each track, and the results. Every adjustment made to the car during practice sessions and races, and the result of each particular adjustment, is noted. They also record track conditions, such as temperature, humidity, whether it is cloudy or sunny, wind direction and speed,

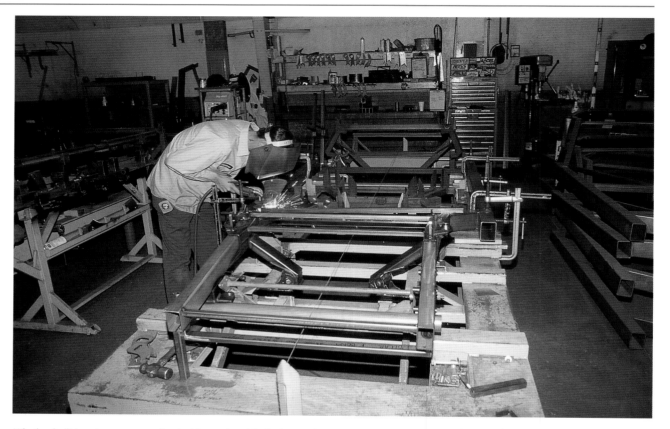

Whether built by a team or a supplier, in this case Laughlin Racing Products, the cradle of a Winston Cup car is the frame fixture. Laughlin Racing Products produces chassis for the Winston Cup Series, the Busch Series, and the Craftsman Truck Series. All of the chassis are built using the same methods.

and so on. Crew chiefs rely heavily on these notes at a race, and the notes they may be looking at may be from a race car that was destroyed in a crash. If the notes are to mean anything, each chassis must be identical (or the crew chief must be aware of any differences built into the chassis) so that he may take them into account when setting up the race car. Thus it is critical that all the cars be built with a high degree of repeatability.

Once the material has been ordered and delivered, the work begins. The first step of the process takes place at the saw. The individual pieces of the chassis are cut to size from stock. Few pieces on the chassis are straight, so most pieces of the chassis must be bent before they are put together. This is accomplished by using hydraulic tube bending machines. The piece of steel tubing is placed onto the machine and a bending tool is selected,

Construction begins with the frame rails being clamped into place. This fixture holds the parts steady and secure while they are being welded together. Once the frame rails have been built, the sheet metal floor pan is tack-welded into place.

based on the desired radius of the bend. Fabricators must pick the point of the bend with great care. It can be a tricky business making multiple bends in a piece of steel tubing and having the final piece be of the proper length and configuration. After the piece has been cut and bent, the ends of the tubing must be prepared for welding. When the piece was cut from stock, the ends were at 90-degree angles, and to be welded, the ends must have either a radius, to fit the outer diameter of a piece of tubing, or an angle, to fit the ends of two or more pieces of tubing. When the piece of tubing has been cut bent and the ends shaped, it is time to see if it fits. If it does, it is welded into place and the next piece is begun.

Four main components make up the chassis: the frame rails, the roll cage, the front subframe, and the rear subframe. The frame rails are the foundation on which all the

A fabricator bolts components into a smaller fixture for welding. After the pieces are fabricated and ready to be welded, they are clamped into place. The fixture, or jig, is the starting point of all of the chassis components. Using fixtures to construct the chassis, builders can build chassis after chassis almost exactly alike. The fixtures allow the builder to proceed with confidence. If the part fits the fixture it is the right size and shape and in the right position. If it does not fit it will not be used, and a mistake will be eliminated.

other components are mounted. This makes the frame rails the "backbone" of the entire chassis. They are the first pieces laid in the chassis assembly process. As the innermost, bottommost frame components of the chassis, they provide the platform for further assembly. The frame rails consist of two side rails, made from magnetic steel box tubing, and must be built parallel with no offsets. These rails are 3 inches wide by 4 inches high, with a minimum wall thickness of 1/8 inch and a minimum length of 65 inches. They must be parallel, with a minimum distance between them of 50 inches, measured from one inside wall to another inside wall. A cross-member 2 inches by 2 inches (1/8 inch thick) must be mounted between the two frame rails to support the rear trailing arms. All of the connections attaching the frame pieces together are welded.

The frame rails then have ballast rails attached to them. These ballast rails hold weights, which may be used to get the car to meet the minimum weight requirements. The teams try to build the cars to be as light as possible. If they are under the minimum weight rule when completed, the team uses ballast to make up the difference. This gives them a little leeway in deciding how the weight is distributed.

Provisions have also been made to factor in the driver's weight. Drivers weighing less than 200 pounds will have weight added to the car in 10-pound increments up to a maximum of 50 pounds. For instance a 175-pound driver will have 30 pounds added. This weight may be added to the left side of the car. After the race, the car must be within 5 percent of the minimum weight of the car at the start of the race.

The ballast rails must be the same size as the frame rails and must be welded to the frame rails. Holes are allowed in the frame, but not if, in the judgment of the officials, they are only to save weight

Once the frame rails have been built, assembly begins on the roll cage. The roll cage is the primary contributor to driver safety. Many feet of steel tubing are blended to achieve one goal—strength. Builders rely on the brute strength of the steel roll cage to prevent injuries from the

Different parts of the chassis are preassembled in different fixtures. Here the roll bar assemblies are built and await their mating to the frame rails. In the event the car gets on its roof, roll bars will be the first and last line of defense.

tremendous impact of collisions with the wall, or other cars, or both. Again, throughout the entire building process of the roll cage, the chassis will stay clamped to the jig. Only when the chassis is complete will it be unclamped from the jig and work begun on another chassis.

The assembly of the roll cage starts at the bottom, building up from the frame rails. Major pieces, such as the main roll bar, are attached to the lower frame first. Connecting pieces are then welded into place between the major structural pieces.

There are many structural bars in a Winston Cup roll cage, including horizontal bars, vertical bars, and a couple of support bars that run diagonally. All of these bars are made from round, magnetic-seamless-steel tubing with a 1-inch diameter and a .090-inch wall thickness (meeting ASTM A-519 specifications).

The C-shaped main roll bar is welded perpendicular to the frame rails, with the open side of the "C" oriented downward and the closed side extending up and across the car. In the event that a car gets on its roof, this will usually be the

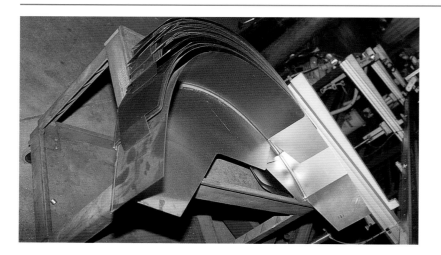

first bar that makes contact with the track. If it slides for any distance on its roof, this bar will take a great deal of abuse. Two additional bars are welded from side to side in the main roll bar. The horizontal shoulder bar is the highest, and as its name implies, it runs at a height about equal to the driver's shoulders. Below it, and running parallel, is the horizontal tunnel bar. The main roll bar is also supported by a diagonal

Some sheet metal parts are prefabricated and added during the assembly of the chassis. Here (left), a supply of rear wheelwells arrives from the sheet metal shop. They are welded into place (below) as a part of the chassis as it would be much more difficult to add them later. Besides the floor pan, the rear fender wells, firewall, and crush panels are welded into place.

bar, which runs from the top driver side to the bottom of the main roll bar on the passenger side.

Other than the main roll bar, two other bars run over the driver's head. The first is the roof bar, another "C"-shaped bar. The backs of the "C" are welded to the main roll bar and the front of the "C" will end in the area of the top of the windshield. The centerline roof bar is then welded into place on the centerline (imagine that) of the car. The front of the bar is welded to the roof bar and the rear end is welded to the main roll cage. Two front roll bar legs attach the roof bar system back to the frame rails. They are welded at the top to the front of the roof line and extend downward, following roughly the same lines as the windshield until they reach its bottom, and then bend downward to run vertically into the frame rails. A dashboard bar is welded into place between the front roll bar legs, positioned in the area of the bottom of the windshield. A center windshield bar is welded, on the centerline of the car, between the dashboard and the front edge of the roof bar. This bar adds structural strength if the car gets on its roof and keeps large pieces of debris, like wheels and tires, from going through the windshield during accidents.

Each side of the roll cage consists of four horizontal door bars. These are welded into place between the main roll bar and the front roll bar leg. Short vertical support bars are then welded into place between the door bars to strengthen them.

Several diagonal bars are incorporated into the roll cage. They are mostly on the right side of the roll cage as the left side must be open for the driver seat.

The final configuration of all of these bars has been developed by both NASCAR and team builders over the years. Accidents on the track show the performance of the bars better than any other test. For instance, until a few years ago there was no center vertical bar behind the windshield. Then there was an accident at Talladega where Dale Earnhardt flipped. While he was on his roof he was hit in the windshield area by the front of another car. This type of impact had never been anticipated and the damage to Earnhardt's car was dramatic. As a result, a new center bar was added, sometimes referred to as the Earnhardt bar.

The firewall, the floor pan, and the rear wheel wells are about the only sheet metal pieces added during the building of the roll cage. Occasionally bars must pass through the sheet metal floor pan to the frame rails. When this happens holes are cut in the sheet metal to allow the bars to pass. All other sheet metal pieces are added after the chassis is completed.

Firewalls are made of 22-gauge steel and must be welded into place. A tunnel is cut through the firewall for the transmission. The tunnel can be no wider than 17 inches at the bottom, and it must be at least 10 inches below the leading edge of the windshield. The tunnel cannot be wider than 10 inches when it passes the driver seat. Firewalls do just what their name implies. They act to protect the driver from the heat of the engine and provide protection during accidents and engine failures. "Crush panels" extend from the firewall to the fenders and also keep heat, fumes, and debris out of the interior of the car. If they are damaged during a race it will be a long afternoon for the driver, as he will get both heat and fumes in the cockpit.

The front subframe is the structure that extends from the firewall to the front of the car. By the rules it must extend from the lower radiator support (in the front) to the forward edge of the front frame rails (in the rear). The mounting positions for the steering and the engine are located on the front subframe. The width of the main subframe rails must be a minimum of 29 inches at the steering box and must be parallel to the centerline of the car. The inside width measured at the engine block may not exceed 34 inches.

Suspension fittings are also built into the front subassembly. For the finished car to handle properly, all of these must be positioned correctly. A mistake at this point could mean a handling problem to overcome on the track. Wire-fed welders are again used to make the connections. Small flanges may be added to provide extra strength

continued on page 77

Above, right and opposite:
Four primary parts make up the chassis— frame rails, roll cage, front clip, and rear clip. The frame rails are the bottommost parts and are the foundation of the entire chassis. The roll cage (above, left) is the center section and its main function is driver protection. The front clip (left) extends forward from the firewall and supports the front suspension as well as providing additional driver protection. The rear clip (above, right) supports the rear suspension, protects the fuel cell, and also helps protect the driver in a "back first" impact.

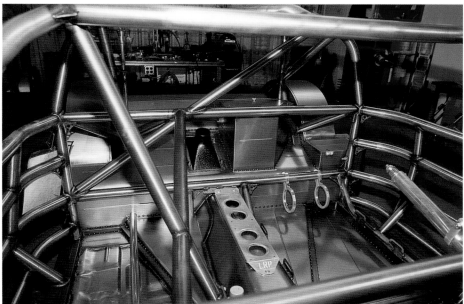

The interior of the car, looking toward the rear. As the chassis nears completion, more and more support bars are added for the driver's protection. Other systems also become visible. Note the mounting points for the fire extinguisher, the oil reservoir tank protective cover, and the air scoop to pick up outside air to cool the oil tank.

When the chassis is complete, it is put on rollers and pushed to the body fabrication shop. If everything was done correctly, the body guys will have a true foundation on which to hang the body. At this point in the construction process, all cars are pretty much the same. In fact, more than one car out there has changed from Ford to Chevy or Chevy to Ford and back again.

Facing page:
During the construction of the chassis, some "nonchassis" parts are installed, in this case, the clutch, brake, and accelerator pedals. These parts are much easier to install before the body has been hung on the chassis.

Facing page, far right:
Small tubes are fabricated and mounted to the chassis for easy access to the track bar and wedge adjustment bolts. These tubes, accessible through holes in the rear window, will guide the wrench directly to the head of the adjusting bolts. Many little parts of the car are easier to add when the chassis is being built.

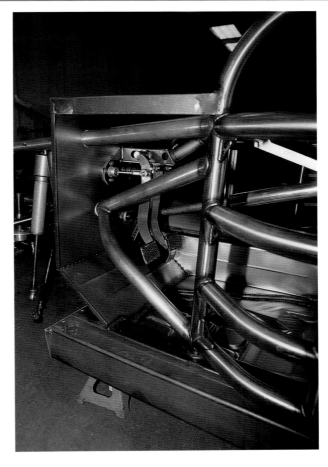

Continued from page 73

around connections. All welded connections must be "clean," with no sharp edges.

The rear subframe extends rearward from the back of the main frame rails, up and over the rear axle and back down to hold the fuel cell. It includes the mounting points for the rear springs, shocks, Panhard bar (track bar), sway bar, and fuel cell. The two sides of the rear subframe are tied together with a 2x3-inch (0.083 inch thick) rail

located a minimum of 8 inches behind the fuel cell. Rear subframe rails must connect to the main frame not less than 57 inches from the front end of the main frame rails. At any point along the rear subframe rails, the distance from the centerline must be the same on each side. The rear subframe must maintain a minimum width of 37 inches at the fuel cell mounting location.

At this point, the bare chassis is complete and is delivered to the next assembly point to have the body mounted and the other components added.

CHAPTER FIVE

Fabricating the Body

As mentioned before, a Winston Cup car may somewhat resemble its street counterpart, but it has few stock parts. The body holds the highest percentage of original factory parts— the hood skin, deck lid skin, and roof skin. I say skins because the stock backing structures have been replaced by custom-made backing structures.

The importance of the body profile has grown in the last two decades of Winston Cup racing. The most critical are the super speedway cars. With the power-robbing restrictor plates on the car, the efficiency with which the car moves through the air determines the car's top speed. At other tracks, the car's body shape will be focused on "downforce." Downforce is the pressure exerted on the body by the air flowing over it, causing the entire car to be pushed down toward the track. This helps the car stick in the turns allowing higher speeds. While downforce helps in the turns, it creates drag when the car goes down the straights. About the only places where the body profile is not critical are the short tracks.

With exception of the roof skin, the front and rear bumper covers, the hood skin, and the rear deck lid skin, the body of the car is handmade and hand-assembled. Fenders, quarter panels, the sides of the car, and many other small body pieces are handmade from standard sheet metal.

The body fabricator begins by selecting a piece of sheet metal from the storage rack. A rough sketch is made directly onto the sheet metal with a marker, and a metal shear is used to cut the rough shape of the part from the large sheet of metal. More precise cuts are then made with hand shears and air-powered clippers.

Once the piece has been cut, it is time to give it some shape. This means adding curves. The compound curves (bending in more than one direction) are very difficult to make and require a great deal of experience to make at all, much less to make them quickly and to make them all the same. Mechanical rollers and English wheels are used to give the part its final contours. These wheels press the metal between two rollers. As the fabricator moves the

Body fabricators know what is waiting for them when they get to the track. Bodies must be built to the exacting standards of the NASCAR rules, which are checked with standardized aluminum templates. If you don't pass this test you will not race.

Much of the body begins life as standard steel sheet metal that can be purchased from any industrial supply house.

Construction of the chassis begins at the top and proceeds downward. Roof height of the final product is strictly inspected every time the car goes on the track. As a result it is on the builder's mind from the beginning. The template is suspended over the car and will remain close by during the building process. The templates used by the team are the same as the ones that they will face during inspection at the race.

piece through the wheels, he applies pressure to the piece causing it to bend.

As a body piece begins to take shape, it is clamped into position on the car to be checked for fit. A steady process of mount-check-adjust begins. A fabricator may go through this routine many times to ensure proper fit.

When the body piece is ready for its final mounting, holes are drilled along the mounting area for the rivets to pass through. Many, many rivets are used to ensure a tight, secure fit. The body must withstand the tremendous air pressure of racing at 200 miles per hour on a super speedway or the "fender banging" so common during short-track racing. The body will deflect debris and withstand some damage, but for protection, the driver relies on the roll cage. Once the rivets have been secured, the edges of the individual body pieces are welded together. Once all of the welding is done, the area is ground smooth.

Some teams receive the chassis already built from a supplier and some build them themselves, but most fabricate their own bodies. At this point in the construction process (the chassis sitting on the floor with no body) all Chevrolets, Dodges, Fords, and Pontiacs are pretty much the same. When the bodies are built onto the chassis, their true identity takes shape.

From the beginning of the building of the body until inspection before the race, the templates rule the body.

Templates are standardized aluminum patterns defining the profile of the car's body. NASCAR establishes the dimensions of the templates, and a car must comply if it is to race.

Body construction begins at the top of the car and proceeds downward. This is done so that the finished height of the car will be correct, and it means that the roof skin is the first piece to go on. By already knowing how high the top of the car is supposed to be when it is completed, builders mount the roof template over the car to use as a guide when building the body. The fabricators hanging the body must make sure that the chassis is positioned perfectly so that the body is hung correctly. To do this the car is usually placed on a surface plate or a fixture, specially built for this purpose. When it is ready, the roof skin is riveted to the roll bars and tack-welded into place.

Next, as the fabricators work from the rear, the rear bumper cover and deck lid are mounted onto the chassis. Then the hood and front bumper cover are added. When this is complete, the builder begins to work downward, adding the fenders, quarter panels, and door areas.

Each part of the body has particular tasks that it must accomplish and special areas that the team must address.

The sheet metal roof, or roof skin, is the same as the one production cars use. Stock roof panels for the make and model car being raced are mandatory. The height, shape, and size of the roof cannot be changed.

Airflow over the roof is also of critical importance. How the air flows off the roof, rear window, and deck lid influences the way the air hits the rear spoiler, which in turn affects the way the car handles. Teams go to great lengths to make sure the airflow to the rear spoiler is optimized while still ensuring that the roof profile remains legal.

Two pieces of aluminum angle (1/2 inch high minimum and 3/4 inch maximum) must be mounted as far to the outside of the roof as possible, between the windshield and the rear glass. These are used to help stabilize the car at high speeds.

The roof flap unit is added at this point in construction. It must be properly aligned to fit well and to function

Above and facing page:
After the roof is secure, the rear deck lid and hood are mounted. Once in place, and in tolerance according to the template, the bumper covers and roof pillars are added.

properly. Roof flaps, which are made to deploy if the car gets sideways or backward in a spin, have become mandatory in Winston Cup racing. When the car gets sideways, the flaps are activated by the low pressure created by air flowing across the roof of the race car. As with an airplane wing, air moving rapidly across the top of the car creates a low-pressure area. When the car gets sideways this low pressure sucks the roof flaps up. Once activated, the flaps "catch" the air under them and push the car down on the

track. This helps keep the air from getting under the rear spoiler and the bottom of the car, which can lift the rear of the car off of the track and result in a very violent accident.

Deck lids (or trunk lids) retain their stock shape, contours, and appearance. When closed they are held shut with two pin fasteners. The deck lid must have working hinges and a self-holding device to keep the lid up when it is open. The deck lid is another one of the few "stock" parts used in a Winston Cup car. The stock deck lid backing

structure is replaced with custom fabricated supports keeping the deck lid rigid at high speeds.

The deck lid is also tethered to the roll bar with cables to prevent it from flying off during a crash. The rear spoiler is mounted on the rear of the deck lid. The air passing over the car and onto the rear spoiler is deflected upward, forcing the rear of the car down and improving the car's handling ability in the turns. This force is commonly referred to as "downforce."

Rear spoilers are nonadjustable and must be attached to the rear deck lid. All spoilers are made of steel, 1/8 inch thick. In an effort to balance the downforce and aerodynamic efficiency of each model of car being raced, NASCAR may mandate different spoiler widths and heights for each model. The

Chevrolet Monte Carlo and Ford Taurus spoilers are 55 inches wide and 6-1/4 inches high. The Grand Prix spoiler is 57 inches wide and 6-7/8 inches high. Spoilers are made in two pieces and mounted with a thin gap on the centerline of the body. This gap is necessary to allow inspection templates to be fitted directly on the car's body when checking the profile. All rear spoilers are made of aluminum and mounted so that they will not bend or flex under the air pressure encountered when racing. Rear spoilers must be mounted with at least six 1/4-inch or larger bolts across the back of the deck lid. Edges must be cut square and the corners can be rounded to no more than a 1/2-inch radius.

At Talladega and Daytona, a predetermined angle setting is used. This setting is determined by officials before

the race, ensuring the angle is high enough to give the cars plenty of downforce, making for safer racing.

Competitors must use the factory-produced hood for the make and model car being raced. Original support panels, used to hold the sheet metal hood rigid, are again replaced with custom supports (fabricated by the teams) made from 1/2 inch by 1/2 inch square material or of 3/8-inch-diameter round magnetic steel tubing. These supports must be strong enough to keep the hood from sagging or deflecting while the car is at speed. The hood must be secured to the roll cage with a 7/32-inch wire rope to keep it from flying off in an accident. The back of the hood is hinged so it opens much like a production car. When closed, the hood is locked into position with four positive pin fasteners (3/8 inch in diameter), which are evenly spaced along the front of the hood. The air intake for the carburetor is located on the centerline of the car, between the back of the hood and front of the windshield.

A clean hood profile is necessary for good airflow over the car. On longer tracks, if the hood is damaged, the

A system of support rods will be fabricated and installed to support the bumper covers. These are made as light as possible, but they must be strong enough to withstand the tremendous air pressure encountered at super speedways and the banging contact of a short-track race.

When the top, front, and rear have been completed, the sides of the car are fabricated. The sides of the car are made up of several pieces, but when complete it will appear as one piece. Each piece is welded together, ground flush, and smoothed with body filler.

disturbance of this airflow will dramatically slow a race car. Short-track performance is usually not affected by cosmetic hood damage.

Factory-produced or aftermarket bumper covers may be used, but they are not the same pieces that are used on production cars. These "one-piece" units are produced for racing purposes only. The dimension and shape of the bumper covers are established before the season begins to ensure that no model gains an unfair advantage by converting the multiple-piece production car bumper to a one-piece racing unit. All bumper covers must have a serial number (which must remain visible), and their shape or contours cannot be altered to improve aerodynamic flow. The front bumper cover is mounted on a frame of square tubing, which is fabricated during the building of the chassis.

Openings are cut in the front bumper cover to allow air to be ducted to various systems that require cooling (primarily brakes and engine). These grill openings are then covered by two layers of wire screen, used for protection from debris. No devices that direct the airflow can be placed between the grill and the radiator.

The grill area is of critical importance and must do a number of things at one time. As the leading edge of the car, the bumper cover is a determining factor in the car's aerodynamic efficiency. Grills must allow enough air to enter to cool the engine, but too large an opening will create drag and will also lift the front end of the car at high speeds, affecting the car's handling. Grill openings are also used to duct air to the brake rotors when racing on tracks that are demanding on brakes (mainly short tracks and road courses). Air is also ducted from the left side of the grill opening to the oil cooler, which is mounted inside the left front fender in front of the left front tire. These systems are likely to overheat if the openings are closed by damage or debris.

The rear bumper covers are manufactured much the same as the front bumper covers. The rear bumper cover's specifications are established by the original equipment manufacturer and NASCAR officials, and it keeps the profile and shape roughly the same as that of a production car.

Often fabricating a body piece turns into a two-man job. Here one fabricator holds a piece of a quarter panel steady while another presses a subtle bend into the sheet metal.

The English wheel is used to roll curves into the sheet metal. It is a simple machine but operating it correctly takes a great deal of training. The pressure of the steel rollers, combined with the fabricator's movement of the sheet metal, results in smooth bends in the piece.

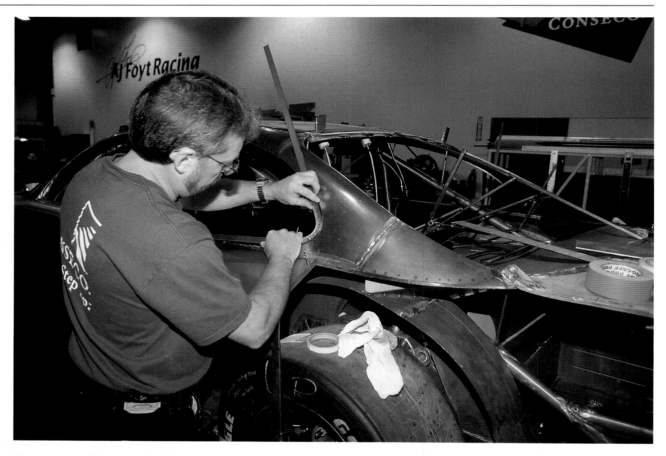

Many, many small pieces must be fabricated from scratch before the car is completed. Here a rail is fabricated to seat a quarter window. It is often all of these little parts that cause the long assembly times when building a body.

The rear bumper cover is of one-piece construction and does not include a functional bumper.

The front air dam must have a minimum ground clearance of 3-1/2 inches. All support brackets holding the air dam in place must be mounted on the back of the air dam. The leading edge of the air dam may not extend more than 1/2 inch forward of the bumper. The total width of any opening in the lower air dam, below the bumper, may not exceed the width of the radiator.

The air dam's purpose is to keep as much air from going under the car as possible. The more air that goes under the car, the more drag and lift the car will have. As

After the body is assembled, it is ready to be sent to the paint booth for a coat of primer. If it is not painted, the steel body will quickly rust. Most of the final assembly will take place while the car is in this state. Often cars are taken to the track and tested before the final paint job is applied.

the car goes faster, the lift increases. If the air dam is damaged on longer, faster courses, the result will be a slower car that is more difficult to drive.

Doors don't really exist on modern Winston Cup cars, although the sides maintain the factory contours and accent lines. They are hand-crafted from sheet steel in one piece, from about the center of the front wheel to the center of the rear wheel although different builder's techniques may vary. The sheet metal pieces are riveted and welded in place, with all weld seams smoothed. A short front fender and rear quarter panel are handmade to fill the areas between the sides and the front and rear bumper covers.

Once painting is complete there is little more to do, other than installing the specific engine, suspension, and drivetrain for the track to be raced.

Due to a lack of doors, the drivers get in and out of the car through the driver side window.

As with all other body pieces on the car, great care is taken in producing the pieces to exacting tolerances. This is more easily said than done, considering the compound curves in the body of a Winston Cup car. When measuring lap speeds down to 1/100 or 1/1,000 of a second, the slightest flaw can upset the aerodynamics of the car and slow it down or affect the handling.

The handmade fenders may be altered somewhat to allow for tire clearance. The stickers are located in precise positions if the car is competing for "manufacturers' awards."

The quarter panel is the body piece that covers the rear tires, running from the back of the door area to the front of the rear bumper cover. The fuel intake is located on the left quarter panel, with a spring-activated valve that opens only when the fill tank nozzle is inserted.

The quarter panel length, when measured from the deck lid seam to the lowest corner, must be 33 inches for the Ford Taurus, 29 inches for the Pontiac Grand Prix, and 30 inches for the Chevrolet Monte Carlo. Inner panels are constructed under the quarter panels to separate the driver compartment from the wheel well.

Even though it is made in a number of pieces, when the assembly process is complete, the entire side of a Winston Cup car is smooth, with no gaps between body panels (with exception of the hood and trunk). Where the sheet metal pieces meet, they are welded together, and any irregularities are worked out before painting. Some extensive bodywork may be necessary to get the body completely slick.

Both the interior and the exterior of the car must be painted before going to the track. A primer coat is put on the car before the final paint is added. Most teams now use a base coat/clear coat system just like production cars. Often after the primer coat is finished, the car is returned

The sheet metal dash is added during the construction of the body.

to the main shop so that assembly can be completed before the final color coat is put on the car. This keeps the paint from being scratched by team members as they are climbing all over the car bolting parts on.

When applying the final paint, the painter must make 10 or 12 cars look exactly the same, so colors must be mixed to exacting standards to ensure consistency.

Once the paint has dried, the team will apply the stickers. Most of the stylish graphics on the cars are stickers, which are much less expensive and time consuming than painting. The rule book governs some decals, such as the car's numbers. Numbers must be at least 18 inches high and located under the door window and on the roof.

Outfitting the Interior

Once the body is completed and the interior painted, it's time to add the "bolt-on" systems to the car, which can be a time-consuming process. One of the first areas to be

addressed is the interior. While a race car's interior is much more Spartan than a production model, there is still a good bit that has to be done. Safety and driver comfort are the main priorities when setting up the interior of the race car.

The dashboard is fabricated out of magnetic steel, and it must be welded into place.

All gauges and controls must be positioned so that the driver can use them with the least distraction to his driving. Gauges are usually mounted so that when all of the needles are pointing straight up, everything is OK, although different drivers like their gauges arranged differently. Teams use "wink type" three-dimensional rearview mirrors with a maximum width of 26 inches. The rearview mirror may not extend outside the car.

The seat in a Winston Cup car is custom fitted to the preference and size of each driver. Obviously height and weight will impact the building of the seat, but the position that individual drivers prefer varies greatly. Some like to sit close to the steering wheel, while others prefer to be farther away. Some like to sit as low as possible in the car, while others like a bit of height. If a team changes drivers, all of the cars will be "reseated" for the new driver. Location of the accelerator, brake, and clutch pedals may also have to be changed, as drivers become very comfortable with a particular positioning and do not like to change. The same goes for the shifter.

Two ignition systems are mounted to the right of the driver. These consist of a primary ignition and a backup system. They are mounted in the cockpit to shield them from both heat and debris. The backup ignition activator switch must be within easy reach.

All roll bars within the driver's reach are padded to help protect the driver during crashes. A complete fire extinguishing system is also installed in the interior. This allows the driver to quickly flood the interior of the car with fire extinguishing chemicals in the case of fire.

Insulating pads are installed along the firewall and floorboard to help insulate the driver from heat. Installing simple parts correctly may sound easy, but more than one car has been slowed by the insulating mat coming loose and "bunching up" under the accelerator. The result is a car that cannot get up to speed because the accelerator can't go to the floor.

The two-way radio is also installed in the cockpit. The driver activates the radio with a button mounted on the steering wheel. Some drivers and crew chiefs talk a good bit. Others seldom use the radio.

All cars must use windshields made of 3/4-inch-thick hard-coated, polycarbonate material. A minimum of three metal braces must be used to support the windshield from the inside of the car. The inside reinforcements are bolted (using 1/4-inch bolts) to the roof or roll bar at the top of the support and to the dash panel at the bottom. The outside reinforcements must be directly in front of the outward, inside supports.

On tracks less than 1.5 miles and road courses, the side windows (or door windows) must be removed. A nylon web screen is installed in the driver-side door window opening. These screens are made of nylon mesh with each strip being a minimum of 3/4 inch wide and a maximum of 1 inch wide. The minimum screen size is 22 inches wide by 16 inches tall. Window screen mounts must be welded to the roll cage.

On tracks more than 1.5 miles, the same screen system is used on the driver window; however, cars must have a full window on the right side of the car. The window must be made of 1/4-inch-thick flat clear polycarbonate and must be one piece. Openings may be cut in the side windows but must follow the same regulations as those cut in quarter windows (listed below). No tape is allowed on the side window glass.

Quarter windows (the small window directly behind the door window) remain located in their stock position. They must also be made 1/4-inch-thick flat clear polycarbonate and must be one piece, although openings may be cut into the quarter windows for cooling systems. They are used to "pick up" air to cool the rear brakes and the oil reserve tank. The maximum hose size for ducting the cool air is 3 inches. No more than two ducts per window are allowed.

The completed interior. Note the ignition systems to the right of the driver. Keeping these in the inside of the car keeps them cool and protected during the race. All of the roll bars within the driver's reach are padded for protection during accidents.

Polycarbonate glass, with a 3/16-inch thickness, is used in the rear and has the same contour and shape as the original glass. No tint in the window is allowed. This ensures that driver's hand signals will be seen when he is waving or pointing to action taking place on the track. He might, for example, be slowing for a pit stop or warning of trouble with the cars ahead. The rear window is secured by two metal straps a minimum of 1 inch wide. These straps are bolted to the roof at the top and to the deck lid support panel at the bottom. Holes are drilled in both sides of the rear window to allow wrenches to be inserted through to the jacking bolts, which adjust the "wedge" or rear spring settings. A secondary air deflector, much like those on the roof, must be mounted on the rear window. It must be a minimum of 1-1/2 inches high and a maximum of 1-3/4 inches high, and is mounted parallel to the cars centerline. It is positioned in line with the left side roof deflector.

CHAPTER SIX

Suspension, Steering, and Brakes

Once the basic shell, the chassis and body, has been built and it has a coat or two of primer, it is pushed to the main assembly area and the installation of all of the bolt-on parts begins. One of the first to be addressed is bolting the suspension under the car. Few things in Winston Cup racing are as important as a properly tuned suspension. Selecting and adjusting the individual suspension components determines the "suspension setup." These setups are the difference between the cars that handle well and win and those that don't handle so well and don't win. There is no doubt that horsepower will get you down the straightaway faster, but the truth is that horsepower is reasonably close between all of the top teams, and the winning race car is usually the one that gets through the corners the fastest. A prime example of this was the result of a 1-inch restrictor plate that was added to the cars at the second race at New Hampshire in 2000. The plate decreased horsepower from over 750 to about 460 (or 40 percent). The pole qualifying speed,

however, dropped less than 5 miles per hour, from 132.089 to 127.632 (or 3.4 percent). It is speed through the turns that makes fast lap times. Take 40 percent of the spring rate out of the car and the speeds would really drop.

Control arms or A-frames are the main link between the chassis and the front suspension. The inside of the upper control arms are mounted to the frame, and they pivot on mounts with heavy-duty bushings. On the outside they are attached to the steering knuckles using balljoints. The lower control arms are attached to the frame and the steering knuckles in the same manner. The front coil spring's lower mount is found on the lower control arms. Winston Cup cars use specially manufactured tubular control arms, which are much lighter and stronger than their stock counterparts. The upper control arm cross-shaft's material must have a minimum diameter of 3/4 inch.

Trailing arms link the chassis and the rear suspension. The fronts of the trailing arms attach to the body

There are good days, bad days, and wreck days. Not all wrecks are caused by a bad setup but many are. If the setup is off it means that the driver's job becomes harder and harder. The bad news is that once a wreck starts it does not discriminate. It will collect good cars and bad cars just the same.

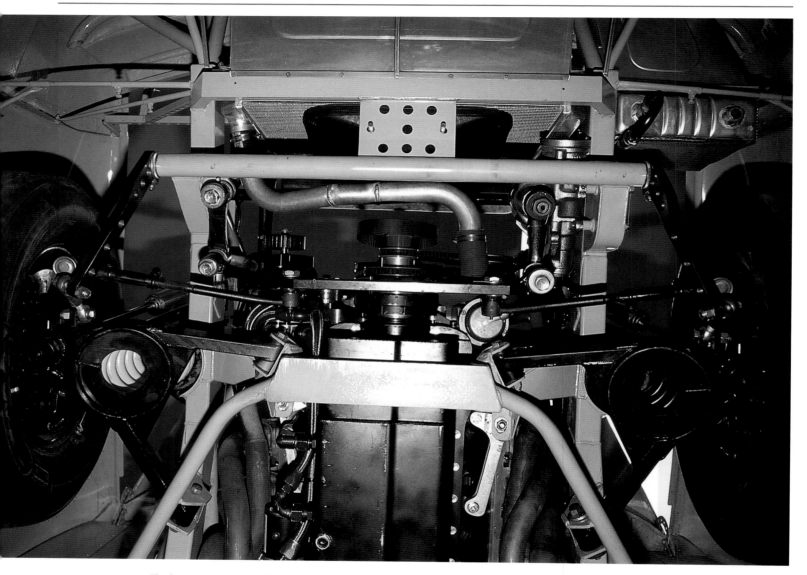

The front suspension of a Winston Cup car incorporates purpose-built components with race-proven aftermarket pieces.

with hinged fixtures just aft of the center of the car. The backs of the trailing arms attach to the rear axle and have fixtures to connect the rear shock absorbers and the rear springs, which are mounted between the trailing arms and the frame.

Winston Cup cars use coil springs on both the front and rear suspensions. Front springs must be heavy-duty magnetic steel with one end closed and one end open and must have a minimum diameter of 5-1/4 inches and a maximum outside diameter of 5-3/4 inches. The front springs mount between the lower control arm and the frame. The bottoms of the springs ride in fittings built into the lower control arms. The top spring mounts are connected to the frame rails.

Rear springs must also be made of heavy-duty magnetic steel, with both ends closed, and must maintain a minimum outside diameter of 4-3/4 inches and a maximum outside diameter of 5-1/4 inches. On the rear suspension the upper and lower coil spring mounts must be located between the rear frame side rails. The rear lower mounts must be located on either the rear axle trailing arms or on top of the rear axle housing. The upper mounts must be connected to the chassis directly above the lower mounts.

Springs are categorized by spring rate, which is a measure of the resistance a spring exerts when compressed, and is measured in pounds of force. Because of the importance of springs in making a car handle well,

continued on page 100

The front coil spring is installed between the lower mount, located on the lower control arm, and the upper mount, located on the frame rail. The top mount, shown here, is attached to a threaded bolt, often called a jack bolt, that runs through a threaded fitting in the frame. Once the spring is installed if this bolt is tightened the spring will be compressed and, presto, more spring pressure. If the bolt is loosened there will be a decrease in spring pressure. This is known as adjusting wedge, and it gives the team a method of changing the spring pressure without changing the springs.

The front sway bar (and the rear) works to stiffen the connection between the body and the suspension. As the car goes into a turn, the body will want to "roll" toward the outside of the turn. You can really feel this effect if you have ever driven a van or an SUV. The sway bars work to stop this, although this link can be set too tight. Drivers may want a little roll as they go through the turn. If they don't have it, the car can become difficult to drive.

While it is set up differently, the rear suspension works much like the front suspension. Unlike many production cars, which use leaf springs, the rear suspension of a Winston Cup car uses coil springs, just like in the front. However, instead of using short control arms like the front suspension, the rear uses long trailing arms. The front of these arms are bolted to fittings just to the rear of the center of the car and run all the way to the rear wheels.

The rear shocks are attached to the rear of the trailing arm on the rear suspension. Unlike many types of race cars that use independent rear suspension, Winston Cup cars all run a solid rear axle.

Braking importance varies from race to race. At big tracks brakes are of little importance and seldom fail. At short tracks they are as important as horse-power, and they can get so hot they can melt a tire. The quickest way to see how important they are at any one track to see how much effort is made keeping them cool. This car is headed for a short track, evident by the three cooling hoses ducted to the left front brake.

Continued from page 97

crews will test many combinations of spring rates on various corners of the car. On all tracks except road courses, a setup will have a different spring rate at each corner of the car to counter the particular forces the track applies to the car as it turns. For instance, at Dover the force on the right front tire is about 3,500 pounds, essentially the entire weight of the car, which forces the team to run a 3,500-pound spring. At a short, flat track there will be much less weight on the right front and the teams will run a much lighter spring.

Even after the team finds the right spring combination of a track, its work is not done. Winston Cup cars are built with fixtures on the upper spring mount that allow the team to tune spring rates even finer. These devices are known as jacking bolts or jackscrews. The bolts have a minimum diameter of 1-1/8 inches, and when they are tightened or loosened they increase or decrease the spring rate. Fans often see this done during pit stops and is most often called "putting wedge in the car" or simply "adjusting the wedge."

Special openings go through the rear window to allow the rear jack bolts to be turned very quickly during pit stops. However, the hood must be opened to adjust the front springs. Rubber inserts are also allowed between the spring coils to add stiffness to the spring. These can be put in or, more commonly, taken out during pit stops to increase or decrease the spring rate.

Winston Cup cars use heavy-duty shocks, similar to the original shocks on the models being raced. Any shock used must be available to all competitors. At one time competitors could run two shocks per wheel but with the recent advances made in shock absorber technology, this is no longer allowed. Modern shock absorbers are able to handle the load with just one shock per wheel. Placing the shocks in the middle of the coil springs is not allowed.

In the last 10 years, teams have begun to spend more and more time finding the perfect shock combination.

This combination in great part determines a car's handling characteristics, and thus its lap times. Shock absorbers are tuned just like most other parts of the car. A "shock dyno" is used to test the shock rebound and handling characteristics. A teams can fine-tune the shock to achieve the compression and rebound combination it desires. This area is closely monitored and shocks are liable to be disassembled and inspected by NASCAR officials. On all cars the rear shocks must be located inside the frame.

Sway bars must be made of magnetic steel. The front sway bar is splined on the end and attached with Heim joints (spherical rod ends). Sway bars function to link the suspension and the chassis/body. The stiffer the sway bar, the tighter the link between the chassis and the suspension. The tighter the link, the less movement between the suspension and the chassis, resulting in less "body roll" when the car is turning. Body roll is just that, the roll of the body when a car is turned. For example, a minivan will roll more in a turn than a Corvette. However, if the sway bars are too stiff, control problems may result. Teams have many sway bar strengths available to allow them to tune the body roll to fit the track being raced.

The track bar is used to keep the rear end "square" under the car. As the car goes through the turn the rear end will be twisted in relation to the body. Track or "Panhard" bars are attached at one end to the frame and at the other end to the end of one of the trailing arms. Usually the bar runs from the left side of the body to the right rear trailing arm. This extra support is critical for stability through the turns. The track bar may be adjusted to refine the handling of the car during both practice and the race.

Winston Cup cars run 9.5x15-inch steel wheels and specially produced racing tires (all of which are supplied by Goodyear). Race tires are of special design and are made of a much softer rubber than even the most radical performance street tires. They have no tread pattern as they are to be used in dry conditions only.

At a super speedway, the thick pads and rotors of the short track are abandoned in an effort to save weight. Everything is lighter, including the rotor, which is thinner, and may have holes drilled in it. The only reason that this is possible is because at tracks like Talladega, the main use of the brakes is to slow and stop the car for servicing during a pit stop.

The friction between the racing surface and the tire heats the rubber, making it even softer. This soft rubber and the tires' heavy sidewall construction allow the cars to achieve such high speeds in the turns.

Tire wear differs depending on the type of track being raced. For safety reasons, tires incorporate an inner liner, a small heavy-duty inner tube mounted on the rim inside the racing tire. In the case of a blowout, this inner-liner should retain its air pressure and keep the rim from digging into the pavement and causing the car to flip. At about $1,500 a set, a team's tire bill can be staggering in itself.

Two terms commonly used to describe tires are "scuffs" and "stickers." "Scuffed" tires have been run for a few laps to "work the tire in." Depending on the track conditions and the setup of the car, teams may scuff new tires during practice to prepare them for use in the race. "Sticker" tires are new tires, which have never been on the car and still have the Goodyear factory sticker on the tire.

Steering knuckles link the suspension to the steering system and both to the wheels. The upper and lower control arms are attached to the steering knuckle's top and bottom using balljoints. The wheel bearings ride on the spindle located on the outward side of the knuckle.

Because of safety concerns, the steering knuckles/spindles must be attached to the frame using steel cables. (Specifically with 5/16-inch wire rope cable constructed of 7x19 stainless steel "aircraft" grade wire, forming a standard Flemish eye mechanical splice at each end secured by a pressed steel sleeve at each eye. A fiber cable made from a continuous loop of 5/16-inch-diameter 12-strand cable woven of Vectran r HS V-12 fiber may be used instead of steel.) This helps keep the entire wheel assembly from becoming detached from the car during crashes.

A "worm"-type gear is used in the steering system, assisted by a power steering pump to help the driver turn the car. Without power steering, you might as well add another "0" to a 500-mile race. When the steering wheel is turned, the gear transfers the circular motion of the steering wheel, through the steering shaft, to the steering gear. The output shaft of the gear is attached to the pitman arm, which changes the circular motion of the wheel into lateral motion. The other end of the pitman arm is attached to the center link. As the center link moves back and forth, the motion is transferred (through tie rods) to the steering knuckles, on which the front wheels are mounted. The idler arm, also attached to the center link, is used to stabilize the center link's movement.

The steering columns used in Winston Cup racing must be made of steel. The center top of the steering post must have 2 inches of resilient material (padding) and a collapsible section must be made into the steering shaft for safety in the event of heavy front impact. Any universal joints used in the steering column, along with the collapsible section of the shaft, must be acceptable to racing officials.

The steering wheel must have steel spokes supporting the rim and a "release system" so the wheel may be removed from the steering column quickly. These quick-release systems make it easier for a driver to get in and out of the car, especially in a crash situation. The driver determines the steering wheel diameter. Each driver chooses a wheel size that gives him the best "feel" when driving the car. Steering wheels are marked so that the driver knows when the wheels are pointed exactly forward. With such a tight fit between the fender and the tire, the tires will not easily come off during pit stops if the wheels are not straight.

Braking capabilities vary widely when dealing with Winston Cup cars. On some tracks, the longer ones, brakes are seldom used. At super speedways, the brakes' biggest job is to slow the car for pit stops. On short tracks and road courses, however, brakes become as important as engine power. Because of this, there are different components for different situations. Super speedway races demand little, so the brakes are as light as possible. Lighter rotors, lighter pads, and no brake cooling. Short tracks demand the other end of the brake spectrum. Heavy rotors, thick pads, and as much cooling as is possible. Rotors used in Winston Cup racing must be made of magnetic cast iron or of cast steel (aluminum mounting hats are allowed). At short tracks, the rotors have to be able to stand up to extreme heat for long periods of time. Brake rotors will continue to work up to approximately 1,200 degrees, which is about the temperature at which they begin to glow. This can be seen at night races at Bristol, as the cars brake hard entering the turn. If the temperature continues to rise, the heat is transferred into the caliper. When this happens, the brake fluid will begin to boil, releasing air into the brake system. A driver will "lose" the pedal when air contaminates the system. Air released into the hydraulic brake system will result in the pedal going all the way to the floor when it is depressed. Because of this, keeping the brakes cool is one of the most critical problems the teams must address. At short tracks and road courses, the car will be set up using thicker rotors.

Cooling is accomplished by ducting air through openings in the body onto the brake components. Cars may have a maximum of three air scoops per brake. Each scoop directs air to the brakes with flexible hose (with a maximum diameter of 3 inches). A 24-square-inch maximum scoop size is allowed. The scoops cannot extend forward of the leading edge of the air dam. Headlight openings may be used for brake cooling, and fans or blowers may be used to increase the airflow to the brakes. Liquid cooling of the brakes, which is used in some forms of auto racing, is not permitted.

Master cylinders on Winston Cup cars are of a simple, non-power-assisted type. They are mounted on the driver side firewall, in roughly the same location as that of production cars. Braking starts at the master cylinder. When the driver presses the brake pedal, the motion actuates the piston in the master cylinder, which applies pressure through the brake lines.

Racing brake lines must be much stronger than their street counterparts. The heat generated at the rotor/pad contact dissipates through the caliper and into the fluid. The fluid, in turn, heats the brake lines. When subjected to such heat, production brake lines can become weak, and the pressure of applying the brakes would cause them to swell. This decreases the pressure to the caliper and makes the entire brake system less efficient. The strength of braided stainless steel lines helps to overcome this problem. Brakes can generate so much heat at short tracks that the heat dissipates through the front-end parts and into the wheel. At times this has been so severe that the tire bead (the part that holds it to the wheel) has melted, causing the tire to come off the wheel—not a good thing at 140 miles per hour.

The brake calipers respond to the pressure of the brake fluid (again, created in the master cylinder by pressing the brake pedal) and squeeze the brake pads against the rotor. This is accomplished by the pressure from the master cylinder being transmitted through the brake line to the caliper. At the caliper, the brake fluid presses against pistons, which press against the brake pads, which in turn "pinch the rotor," slowing the car down. Most street car calipers have one or two pistons per caliper, while Winston Cup calipers have four pistons per caliper, allowing more pressure to be applied to the pads more evenly. Like the other components, racing calipers must be built to stand up to the incredible heat generated when braking hard.

Brake pads are made especially for the purpose of racing. Due to the extreme heat encountered in racing brakes, most normal street pads would wear out far too quickly. Instead of being made predominantly of an organic material, racing pads are a carbon/metal mix, which is much more heat and wear resistant.

CHAPTER SEVEN

Engine and Drivetrain

While victory is usually a matter of handling, horsepower never hurts. Drivers love to out-handle other cars in the straightaway, meaning they have more engine power. With the strict rules, and the tendency for engine builders to change teams, the horsepower war is surprisingly equal between the top teams.

Each engine begins life as a raw block. Only small-block V-8 engine blocks are allowed, and while there are many small blocks of different configuration and displacement out there, for both Ford and General Motors, the NASCAR rules only allow the following blocks. For Chevrolet it is the 350-cid and for Ford the 351-cid. The maximum compression allowed is 12:1 in any cylinder. The formula for determining the cubic inch displacement of each cylinder is Bore X Bore X 0.7854 X Stroke. Once this had been calculated for each cylinder, the results are added together to get the total engine displacement. A "cool down" period, a maximum of three hours, is allowed before the cid is to be inspected by NASCAR officials.

Each car must run the engine of its make, meaning you can't put a Ford engine in a Chevrolet. The motor cannot be located farther back than with the centerline of the forward-most spark plug hole on the right side cylinder head in line with the upper balljoint. Also, the centerline of the crankshaft must be on the centerline of the tread width (equidistant from both front wheels). A minimum of 10 inches of ground clearance is mandatory from the center of the crankshaft to the ground. All motor mounts must be made of steel and are not adjustable.

The racing divisions of General Motors and Ford manufacture the blocks used in Winston Cup Racing. These blocks are made specifically for racing and do not appear in any production vehicle. The material used in making blocks is cast iron. Aluminum blocks are not allowed.

Engines may start with a longer stroke and smaller cylinder diameter. As a block is worn and is bored out, the stroke is shortened as the bore increases to achieve the desired displacement. By using this method, blocks can be

Horsepower is not the key to speed but it sure helps. The trick is getting the suspension to the point where the power can be applied. If a car handles badly the driver will not be able to use all of the engine's horsepower. At some tracks, if a car's setup is right, the car can hold its position even if it loses a cylinder.

Above and facing page:
The foundation of any motor is the block. (Above) The bottom of the block with the main bearing caps bolted into place. Winston Cup blocks have "four-bolt mains," meaning that four bolts secure each bearing cap. Most production cars only have two bolts securing the caps. (Facing page) The top of the block shows the cylinder bores and the machined head mating surfaces.

used for a relatively long period of time. Some two- and three-year-old blocks are still racing. Racing blocks differ from the production blocks in that they have thicker cylinder walls to eliminate distortion and give a better surface for the rings. Improved water passages increase the cooling ability. Adding bulkhead material to the main bearing bosses adds strength around the crankshaft. Increased strength around the deck surface where the heads bolt on increases engine stability. Both Ford and Chevrolet blocks have four-bolt main bearing caps.

When working on a block the following may not be changed: the material, the number of cylinders, the angle of the cylinders, the number and type of main bearings, the location of the camshaft, and the overall configuration.

Assembly of the engine begins with the bottom end, which means first bolting in the crankshaft. The power of the motor is collected and transmitted by the crankshaft. It bears the brunt of the combustion in the cylinder, turning the downward motion of the piston into a rotary motion, with the help of the connecting rods. The crankshaft pro-

vides the motion and power to push the piston back to the cylinder head for the next go around.

Most crankshafts are alloy steel forgings, made by aftermarket sources. Only magnetic steel crankshafts are allowed. Crankshafts may be lightened and balanced, and approved harmonic balancers (bolt-on balancing devices) are also allowed. The crankshaft lobes are tapered on the leading edges to reduce windage, the drag created by the front edge of the crankshaft lobes passing through the air and oil in the block, allowing the engine to spin more easily, and increasing horsepower.

Some areas of the inside of the block can be lined with epoxy fillers. This helps facilitate good oil flow through the block and will result in a few more horses.

The crankshaft is installed and the main caps are bolted into place. Next, the pistons and rods will be added. One piston and rod have already been installed into this motor. The bottom rod cap is visible on the left side of the crankshaft.

A set of rods, rod bolts, and piston wrist pins wait their turn to go on the motor. While qualifying motors may run a lighter rod, engine builders typically use a heavy rod for the race. A few horsepower is not worth the chance a rod will break halfway through a race.

Teams use various brands of high-quality bearings, and engine builders may take quite a long time installing main bearings, making sure of a tight, clean fit.

Connecting rods connect the piston to the crankshaft. Only solid magnetic steel connecting rods are allowed. Most are forged, H-beam style rods that are heavy and very strong. Engine builders tend not to give up much on the rods, not wanting to risk strength for a small performance gain. Heavy rod bolts are used to attach the rod caps. Many Chevrolets and Fords use identical rods. No stainless steel or titanium rods are allowed.

In any motor, pistons perform two tasks. When moving downward in the cylinder on the power stroke, they transmit the energy of the combustion to the crankshaft. They behave much like a bullet does when moving down the barrel of a gun as a result of the hot expanding gas of the ignited gunpowder. Unlike a bullet, the piston has to change direction at the end of the barrel and move back the other way. When the piston moves upward on the exhaust stroke, it forces the spent gases out the exhaust port in the cylinder head.

Winston Cup cars may use any type of round aluminum piston. Most are forged aluminum. Pistons take an incredible pounding during 500 miles of racing. With the high compression and intense combustion pressures experienced in a racing engine, pistons will occasionally fail, usually burning a hole through the top of the piston. (This is what is meant by "burning a piston.")

Pistons used in Winston Cup racing are not "flat topped." The crowns of the pistons have domes, which help to increase compression. They must be "fly-cut" or "relieved" to provide clearance for the valves, which share space in the combustion chamber with the piston domes. When the valves are off their seats, they cannot contact the rising piston or the engine will self-destruct.

All Winston Cup cylinder heads are aluminum. Recent changes in the rules have limited the available heads to one Ford and one General Motors head design. Heads must be one of these:

For Ford Cars	For GM Cars—
Ford E3ZM6049C3	**The SB2 head,**
(dated 9/9/91 or later)	GM 12480011

Valve location and angle must remain stock. Spacing between valves (center to center) is 1.935 inches for Chevrolet and 1.900 inches for Ford. Internal polishing and "porting" (custom machining the intake and exhaust ports on the cylinder head to match the manifold ports) are allowed. Before this rule, many more types of cylinder heads were available. As they were modified more and more, a team could easily have $20,000 to $30,000 in a set of heads. The new rules strictly limit the modifications allowed, which in turn ensures that the heads will

be less expensive, more durable, and that racing will remain competitive.

Now the rules governing the heads are much tighter. The following may not be changed when working a cylinder head: the material, the number of valves per cylinder, the type of combustion chamber, the location of the spark plugs, the orientation of the spark plugs, the arrangement of the valves, the type of valve actuation, the angle of the valves, the number of intake ports, the number of exhaust ports, the center distances of intake ports referenced to the cylinder bore, the center distances of exhaust ports referenced to the cylinder bore, the shape of ports at mating surface of manifolds, the angle of the port face relative to the mating surface of head to block, and the firing order.

The cam is the mechanical brain of the engine. It rotates, getting its power from the crankshaft by means of the timing chain. As the camshaft rotates, the lobes on its surface act (with the lifters, pushrods, and rocker arms) to open and close the valves. The distance the lifter and pushrod move is known as lift, and the time it stays open is the duration. Lift is measured in inches. (A .600-inch cam has a lobe height of .600 inch.) Duration is measured in degrees. (A 270-degree cam holds the valve open for 270 degrees of its rotation.) Different lifts and durations can dramatically change the power band of an engine. The quicker the valve opens and the longer it stays open means more intake and exhaust and more power. But it also means more angle on the lobe and more chance of failure. As a result, engine builders must seek a cam that strikes a balance between durability and an acceptable amount of power.

A camshaft has to be many things at once. A cam has to be hard in the lobe area for resistance to friction, but must be "soft" enough to flex a little and not be brittle, which may cause the camshaft to crack and then and break completely.

It is very difficult to produce a camshaft that fits all of these requirements. Camshaft durability is so important that teams may run the same camshaft at many different (nonrestrictor plate) tracks, relying on intake ports, headers,

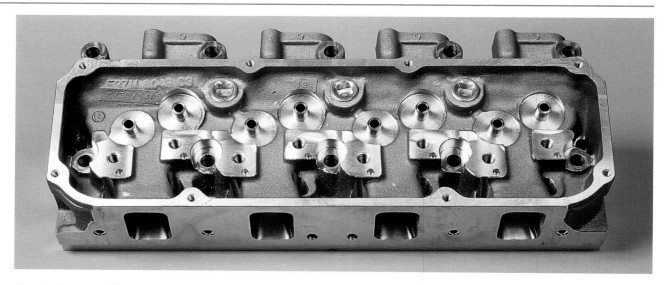

Once the "bottom end" of the motor has been assembled, the cylinder heads are bolted on. (above) The top of the cylinder head, showing the openings for the valves and the machined area where the valve springs ride. (below) The bottom of a cylinder head, showing the combustion chamber and the valve seats. These seats ensure a tight fit when the valve is in the closed position.

and intake manifolds to change the "power band" of the engine to fit the particular track.

Teams may use any magnetic steel flat-tappet camshaft, and it must have the same direction of rotation as the NASCAR-approved production engine.

Lifters ride in cylinders located on the top of the block. The bottom of the lifter sits on the camshaft lobes, transferring the "lift" of the lobe (through the pushrod) to the rocker arm. Only solid magnetic steel, or steel-hydraulic, flat-tappet, barrel-type lifters are allowed. This rule eliminates "roller lifters," which incorporate a rolling tip that rides against the cam, reducing friction and allowing much more radical lobe designs. Mushroom lifters, or any lifter that assists in closing the valve, are not allowed. Maximum lifter size allowed on both GM and Ford is .875-inch diameter.

Pushrods are a high-quality racing type, able to withstand the tremendous force within the valvetrain. They too must be magnetic steel. Guide plates are allowed to help support the pushrods.

The rocker arms transfer the upward movement of the pushrod into a downward movement, providing the pressure to open the valves. Teams use roller-bearing rocker arms of a "split shaft" design, which are much stronger than production rocker arms. Unlike many stock rocker arms, these have a roller tip that eliminates friction at high rpm.

Valves are the "doors" to the individual cylinders, through which (hopefully) only the fuel-air mixture and exhaust flow. Only magnetic steel and titanium valves are allowed in Winston Cup Racing, and there is no restriction on either intake or exhaust valve size. Valve location and angle, however, must remain stock. As a practical matter, the specification of the "legal" cylinder head dictates the maximum size of the valve seats. There is little room to increase the valve size within these parameters. A maximum of two valves per cylinder is allowed.

Valves springs hold the valve closed when it is not being forced open by the rocker arm. They are made from high-quality magnetic steel, and as engine speeds have increased, valve springs have become difficult parts to manufacture. Winston Cup engine speeds have increased to the point where turning over 9,000 rpm is common. Harmonic problems at a particular rpm cause many valvetrain problems. Staying at an rpm where the point of bad harmonics occurs will increase the chances of engine failure. This is especially a problem at longer tracks where engines run a long time in one rpm range. Engine builders try to predict the point of bad harmonics, and design the engine so that these areas are in an rpm range that is not sustained. As the engine accelerates or decelerates through this range, harmonics are usually not a problem.

The fuel-air mixture that ultimately flows through the intake valves begins with air "picked up" through the intake at the rear of the hood. From this aperture, the air enters the air filter housing. All Winston Cup cars use a round, dry-type air filter, much the same as the one used on production vehicles. The mandatory minimum diameter is 14 inches, and the maximum is 16 inches. Air filter housings are made of composite materials or metal. The top and bottom pieces must be the same diameter and must be centered on the carburetor. The air filter element must be from 1-1/2 inches to 4 inches high. Air filters may not be removed either during the race or during practice.

Once the air has been filtered, it enters the carburetor, where it is mixed with fuel. Winston Cup cars run four-barrel, mechanically advanced, secondary venturi carburetors. Some polishing and other minor internal changes are allowed, but no external alterations are made. Carburetor jets must be the same type as supplied by the manufacturer. Carburetors and their use are monitored closely by racing officials.

Restrictor plates, mounted between the carburetor and the intake manifold, are used at Talladega and Daytona to limit the amount of fuel-air vapor to the engine. The result is less air, lower rpm, less horsepower, and lower speeds. The following models are the only carburetors allowed.

Once the cylinder heads are bolted on (with the valves and valve springs already installed), the rest of the valvetrain is assembled. Here the engine builder is installing push rods and rocker arms. All of these parts can be seen in the tray on top of the intake manifold. Note that the manifold, alternator, pulley systems, and oil pump have already been installed.

On all tracks except Talladega and Daytona:
Holley 4150 Series with 1-9/16-inch maximum venturi and 1-11/16-inch maximum throttle bore.
At Talladega and Daytona:
Holley 4150 Series with 1-3/8-inch maximum venturi and 1-11/16 -inch maximum throttle bore.

When reworking carburetors, only Holley replacement parts may be used.

When the fuel/air mixture exits the carburetor, it flows through the intake manifold to the cylinder head. High-performance aluminum intake manifolds are used in Winston Cup racing. The manifold used must be a model that has been approved by NASCAR officials. There are currently five approved intake manifolds for both Ford and General Motors:

Ford	General Motors
Edelbrock 2961	Edelbrock 2923
Edelbrock 2991	Edelbrock 2963
Ford M-9424-A351	GM 2480048
Ford M-9424-E351	GM 12370854
Ford M-9424-W351	GM 1240000

Different intake manifold modifications mix the fuel-air mixture coming from the carburetor in different ways, making the same engine run differently. Epoxy fillers may be added to the individual runners to change the flow characteristics of the manifold. Fillers may not be added to the plenum floor or walls. The intake opening size must be at least 3-9/16 inches when measured front-to-back, and 3-5/8 inches when measured side-to-side.

Once the fuel-air mixture has been burned, the remains are flushed from the cylinder, through the exhaust port and into the exhaust system. The exhaust system is made up of three main components: the headers, the collector pipe, and the exhaust pipes.

Headers are made from pipe, bent to a custom fit. Each pipe runs from the exhaust port on the cylinder head to the collector pipe. By making each individual piece the same length, the exhaust system will help "pull" the exhaust gases from the cylinder, increasing engine efficiency. The shape, length, and configuration of the header pipes can be adjusted to tune the power band of the engine. This allows engine builders to custom tailor the car's power band to each track, building the maximum power where it is needed the most.

Collector pipes combine the four individual header runners on each side of the engine into a common pipe. Collector pipes are the links between the individual header runners and the single exhaust pipe.

Exhaust pipes begin at the collector pipe and must exit the car at the side between the front and rear wheels. They may exit the car on either side but often teams locate both pipes on the left side of the car. This eliminates the chance that they might be "pinched" shut as the car pitches over in left-hand turns or makes contact with the outside wall. Exhaust pipes may have a maximum 3-1/2-inch inside diameter and must extend past the driver, under the frame and to the outer edge of the car. They cannot be fitted into a notched area in the rocker panel, quarter panel, or frame, and they must be secured to the car with at least two 1/8-inch by 1-inch steel U-shaped brackets.

The exhaust pipes are not round. Instead they are "flattened," giving more ground clearance (which must be a minimum of 3 inches).

Keeping a Winston Cup engine cool is a bit more complicated than keeping a production engine cool. Winston Cup cars run a "dry sump" oil system, which is

Above and facing page:
Unlike a production engine, in which the oil system is contained within the engine, a Winston Cup car has oil moving all over the car. The high-volume pump moves the oil through an oil cooler, which is a small radiator located behind the left front fender, and an oil reservoir tank located behind the driver. This system allows the teams to run more oil in the system and keeps it cooler.

not found on production vehicles. Instead of the oil flowing down to the pan to be recycled through the engine by a pump (that picks up the oil from the bottom of the oil pan), the dry sump system keeps the oil in motion at all times. The pump is mounted on the outside of the engine (much the same as an alternator is mounted) and is driven by a belt. After the oil runs through the engine, it is quickly "picked up" from the bottom of the oil pan and pumped back into the oil system. During circulation the oil passes through many feet of hose, an oil tank mounted in the left rear of the car and an oil cooler mounted in the left front of the car.

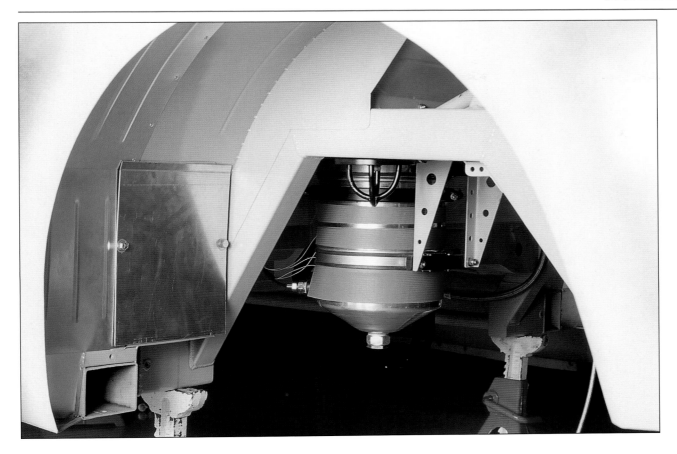

The system runs at about 70 to 80 psi, and an acceptable range of oil temperature is 250 to 270 degrees Fahrenheit. With modern engine speeds, proper oil cooling is essential to be competitive on the track.

Mounted behind the driver, the oil reserve tank holds approximately 18 quarts of oil. It must be encased in a leakproof, insulated 22-gauge metal box. Oil reserve tanks are always located behind the driver, putting the weight in the middle and on the inside of the car. Due to this positioning, great care is taken to make the tank and protective shield as tough as possible. An extra oil temperature gauge is located on the oil reservoir tank so that crewmen can quickly get a read on the oil temperature.

The oil cooler is a radiator used to keep engine oil cool. Oil constantly circulates through the cooler and as with a coolant radiator, the air (entering through the left front grill opening) is forced through the cooling fins, and the oil circulating through the passageways is cooled.

Mounted in the left front corner of the car, the oil cooler is a fairly vulnerable piece of equipment. Often a Winston Cup car cannot survive impact to the left front that might be survivable to the right front because of the oil cooler.

The final products of the engine room are lined up and ready to be put on the transporter and taken to the track. With qualifying motors, practice motors, race motors, and backups, a team may carry as many as a half-dozen engines to each race.

Winston Cup cars use oil filters very much like those on production cars. But instead of being attached to the engine, the oil filter is mounted in the engine well, in a very accessible position. Only high-quality stainless steel braided line is used for the oil system, due to the high temperature and the consequences of a line failure.

Winston Cup oil pumps are mounted onto the engine in much the same way that an alternator is mounted. Power is transferred to the oil pump by a wide heavy-duty belt running off of a special crankshaft pulley. These heavy-duty pumps have a high pumping output in order to push the oil quickly throughout the system. The pump's body must not exceed 9-1/2 inches in length and 3-1/2 inches in crosssection.

Winston Cup cooling systems are similar to their production counterparts but with a few modifications. No special systems that use ice, Freon, or any other coolant can be used. Cooling is of critical importance to a Winston Cup engine.

With the 12:1 compression ratings being run and the high engine speeds being turned, much more heat is generated than in a production engine. Only high-strength hoses are used in the cooling system. For example, the lower radiator hoses are most often one-piece metal pipes. Other hoses are braided stainless steel with special high-pressure fittings. Any hose failure on the track means a hazardous wet spot for all of the drivers to go through, so hose integrity is of prime importance.

Winston Cup cars all use aluminum radiators. Radiators are stock appearing and mounted in the stock position, not exceeding 2 inches from vertical. Dust screens are fabricated to prevent debris from entering the radiator. The radiator overflow pipe can be relocated to an alternate position.

One of the biggest problems with radiators during the race is clogging, the result of small pieces of tire rubber ground off the cars during racing. These small gooey pieces become stuck inside the fins of the radiator, impairing its ability to pass air and cool the fluids.

The clutch is the link between the engine and the drivetrain. Most "stock" clutches will only have one disc. A Winston Cup car runs a three- or four-disc clutch. This gives the clutch more disc surface, which increases its grip.

Winston Cup cars run a specially built mechanical water pump. Again, because of the heat generated in a Winston Cup engine, more water pump output is needed than a stock pump can provide. The impeller that does the actual pumping may be altered, changing the pitch and shape to change coolant flow rates. Changing impellers can greatly increase the pumping ability of the cooling system, and this increased circulation will improve the cooling efficiency of the entire system.

Teams may use either engine-mounted fans or electric fans. If engine-driven, the fan must be steel with no fewer than four blades. The pitch of the blade can be changed to increase or decrease the airflow. All fans must have a diameter of at least 14 inches. Individual blades on the fan must be at least 3-1/2 inches wide. Fans must be operational and must be driven by a standard type of belt from the crankshaft or by an electric motor. Today, teams tend to run electric fans. These fans draw less energy from the engine by using an electric motor to turn the blade instead of a belt drive.

Winston Cup cars use mechanical fuel pumps. Mechanical pumps get their pumping energy from a push rod actuated by a lobe on the camshaft. For safety reasons, electric fuel pumps are not allowed in Winston Cup racing. If an engine with a mechanical pump quits running, the fuel quits pumping. However, in a car with an electric fuel pump, the fuel may keep pumping even if the engine quits running. In a crash situation, this could be disastrous.

Fuel line is a high-quality stainless steel braided type, which is rated to a much higher pressure than regular fuel line, and is also much more resistant to damage and wear.

Instead of a regular production gas tank, Winston Cup cars are required to use a "fuel cell." Fuel cells have a plastic body much stronger than a stock tank and much harder to damage. They are also partitioned so that in the event of a rupture the fuel will not gush out of the opening. The fuel cell is encapsulated in a heavy steel cage in the rear subframe.

Electronic ignition systems are used in Winston Cup racing, but computerized systems are not allowed. The major ignition system components are located in the cockpit, to the right of the driver to protect the components from debris and heat. All cars have two separate ignition systems, with two electronic ignition controls and two coils, which are mounted side by side in the cockpit. In the event of an ignition failure, the driver can quickly flip a switch, changing to the backup system without having to make a pit stop.

Distributors are mounted in the stock location and maintain the firing order of the stock model being raced. High-quality aftermarket distributors and heavy-duty plug wires are used, and every car has a functioning alternator. The alternators must work within preset specifications. Only standard drive belts are allowed. The battery is located in a box mounted behind the driver, in a compartment accessed through a door in the front of the left rear wheelwell. A standard high-quality 12-volt automotive battery is used. Winston Cup cars all have working starters. After a race is under way, a car may be "push started" in the pits, but a car may never be pushed onto the track.

Drivetrain

The flywheel, located at the rear of the engine, is bolted to the crankshaft to dampen vibration and smooth the power of the engine. The flywheel enhances the inertia of the engine and keeps it spinning once the rpm rise. Flywheels must be solid and made of steel. Drilling holes to lighten them is not allowed. The starter ring is located on the outside edge of the flywheel and must maintain a minimum outside diameter of 12-7/8 inches.

The clutch transmits the power from the engine to the drivetrain. Discs ride against the flywheel, picking up power, which is transmitted on to the input shaft of the transmission. Multiple-disc clutches are permitted in Winston Cup racing. Pressure plates and discs must be steel. The minimum clutch diameter allowed is 7-1/4 inches. Most teams use a three- or four-disc system with small diameter discs. Even though the discs are smaller than those in stock clutches, these multidisc clutches have much more surface area; thus, they will stand up to the extreme strains of a 750-horsepower engine. Longer tracks can be hard on clutches, mainly when the car leaves the pits. Due to the rear gear ratios needed to reach the higher speeds on the super speedway, starting in first gear from a dead stop in a super speedway car is like starting in second gear in a street car.

Aftermarket four-speed transmissions are used in all of the cars. With the exception of road courses and Pocono, drivers usually only shift when exiting the pits. On oval tracks, the cars are geared so that they can stay in fourth gear all of the way around the track.

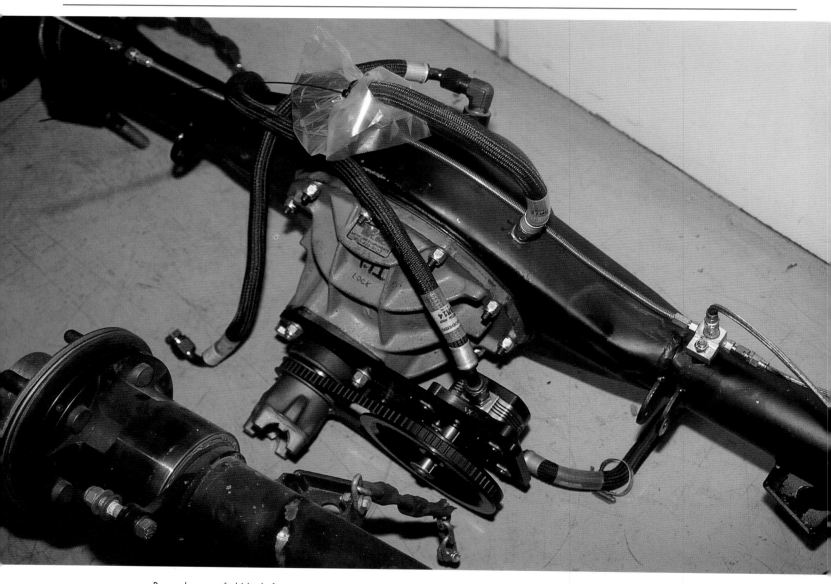

Rear axles are refurbished after every race. Note the pump assembly used to circulate the oil through the rear gear. This keeps the gear cooler and greatly reduces the chance of failure.

Teams may use only special clutch housings. A 3/8-inch steel scatter-shield is mandatory. The scatter-shield is an important piece of equipment. At the high rpm that the engines turn, a broken clutch component or flywheel can become a very dangerous projectile—not only dangerous to the driver in the car but also to the other drivers on the track. The scatter-shield works to contain any breakaway components, preventing them from being released to do damage.

Winston Cup cars use special aftermarket four-speed transmissions. All forward and reverse gears must be operational. If a gear in the transmission fails after the race begins, the car may continue racing. No automatic or semiautomatic transmissions are allowed. Transmissions must be standard shift with an "H" pattern.

Driveshafts are similar in design to standard production types. Two steel brackets are placed around the driveshaft and attached to the floor or cross-member, preventing the driveshaft from dropping to the track in case of failure. Driveshafts must be painted white so that if the brackets fail, the driveshaft can be seen lying on the track.

Different tracks require different rear-end gear ratios to ensure that all of the engine power available is optimized. An example of a rear gear ratio is 4.11:1 (read 4.11 to 1). This means that the driveshaft turns 4.11 revolutions for every 1 revolution of the tire.

All Winston Cup cars, even Chevrolets, use a Ford 9-inch design. Only one-piece magnetic steel housings are allowed.

A cooling system is often used to keep the gear oil in the rear end cool. It works much like the oil cooling system but on a smaller scale. The oil is pumped from the rear end, cooled, and then is returned back to the gear.

Examples of possible gear ratios at a few different tracks:

Atlanta	3.64:1
Bristol	5.25:1
Charlotte	3.70:1
Darlington	3.90:1
Daytona	2.94:1
Dover Downs	4.11:1
Indianapolis	4.20:1
Martinsville	6.20:1
Michigan	3.70:1
New Hampshire	3.60:1
Rockingham	4.22:1
Phoenix	4.22:1
Pocono	3.89:1
Richmond	4.86:1
Sears Point	5.30:1
Talladega	2.94:1
Watkins Glen	3.89:1

Conclusion

Every week of the year, the teams build cars. They pour a little of themselves into each one. A few cars will win. Most won't. Many will head back from the race with damage. Some are totaled. Nevertheless the teams will build more. Either way, it is back to the shop. With the competition as fierce as it is in Winston Cup racing, two areas of racing must be mastered. One is the race on the track. The guys at the track—driver, crew chief, and pit crew—will handle this. The other race is in the shops. It is the race to build more power, better handling and dependability into the car. If the entire team is not successful in this race, the guys at the track won't have a chance.

Appendix: Team List

Dale Earnhardt Inc.
Car Number   1
Driver   Steve Park
Location   1675 Coddle Creek Highway
                  Mooresville, NC
Crew Chief   Paul Andrews
Car Owner   Dale Earnhardt Inc.
Primary Sponsor   Pennzoil
Make of Car   Chevrolet Monte Carlo

Penske Racing South
Car Number   2
Driver   Rusty Wallace
Location   136 Knob Hill Road
                  Mooresville, NC
Crew Chief   Robin Pemberton
Car Owner   Roger Penske
Primary Sponsor   Miller Lite
Make of Car   Ford Taurus

Richard Childress Racing
Car Number   3
Driver   Dale Earnhardt
Location   236 Industrial Drive
                  Welcome, NC
Crew Chief   Kevin Hamlin
Car Owner   Richard Childress
Primary Sponsor   GM Goodwrench Service Plus
Make of Car   Chevrolet Monte Carlo

Morgan-McClure Motorsports
Car Number   4
Driver   Robby Gordon
Location   26502 Newbanks Road
                  Abingdon, VA
Crew Chief   David Ifft
Car Owner   Larry McClure
Primary Sponsor   Kodak MAX Film
Make of Car   Chevrolet Monte Carlo

Hendrick Motorsports
Car Number   5
Driver   Terry Labonte
Location   4433 Papa Joe Hendrick Blvd.
                  Harrisburg, NC
Crew Chief   Gary DeHart
Car Owner   Rick Hendrick
Primary Sponsor   Kellogg's
Make of Car   Chevrolet Monte Carlo

Roush Racing
Car Number   6
Driver   Mark Martin
Location   122 Knob Hill Road
                  Mooresville, NC
Crew Chief   Jimmy Fennig
Car Owner   Jack Roush
Primary Sponsors Viagra/Pfizer
Make of Car   Ford Taurus

Ultra Motorsports
Car Number   7
Driver   Mike Wallace
Location   6007 Victory Lane
                  Harrisburg, NC
Crew Chief   Tim Brewer
Car Owner   Jim Mattei
Primary Sponsor   NationsRent
Make of Car   Chevrolet Monte Carlo

Dale Earnhardt Inc.
Car Number   8
Driver   Dale Earnhardt Jr.
Location   1675 Coddle Creek Highway
                  Mooresville, NC
Crew Chief   Tony Eury Sr.
Car Owner   Dale Earnhardt Inc.
Primary Sponsor   Budweiser
Make of Car   Chevrolet Monte Carlo

Evernham Motorsports
Car Number   9
Driver   Bill Elliot
Location   Harrisburg, NC
Crew Chief   TBA
Car Owner   Evernham Motorsports
Primary Sponsor   Dodge
Make of Car   Dodge Intrepid R/T

MBV
Car Number   10
Driver   Johnny Benson
Location   6780 Hudspeth Road
                  Harrisburg, NC
Crew Chief   James Ince
Car Owners   Tom Beard/Nelson Bowers
                  II/and Read Morton
Primary Sponsor   Valvoline
Make of Car   Pontiac Grand Prix

Brett Bodine Racing
Car Number   11
Driver   Brett Bodine
Location   304 Performance Road
                  Mooresville, NC
Crew Chief   Greg Ely
Car Owner   Diane Bodine
Primary Sponsor   Ralph's
Make of Car   Ford Taurus

Penske-Kranefuss Racing
Car Number   12
Driver   Jeremy Mayfield
Location   163 Rolling Hills Road
                  Mooresville, NC
Crew Chief   Peter Sospenzo
Car Owners   Michael Kranefuss/Roger Penske
Primary Sponsor   Mobil 1
Make of Car   Ford Taurus

AJ Foyt Racing Ltd.
Car Number   14
Driver   Ron Hornaday
Location   128 Commercial Drive
                  Mooresville, NC
Crew Chief   Philippe Lopez
Car Owner   A.J. Foyt
Primary Sponsor   Conseco
Make of Car   Pontiac Grand Prix

Dale Earnhardt Inc.
Car Number   15
Driver   Michael Waltrip
Location   1675 Coddle Creek Highway
                  Mooresville, NC
Crew Chief   TBA
Car Owner   Dale Earnhardt Inc.
Primary Sponsor   NAPA
Make of Car   Chevrolet Monte Carlo

Roush Racing
Car Number   17
Driver   Matt Kenseth
Location   Highway 49 South
                  Liberty, NC
Crew Chief   Robbie Reiser
Car Owners   Jack Roush/Mark Martin
Primary Sponsor   DeWalt Tools
Make of Car   Ford Taurus

Joe Gibbs Racing Inc.
Car Number   18
Driver   Bobby Labonte
Location   13415 Reese Blvd. West
                   Huntsville, NC
Crew Chief   Jimmy Makar
Car Owner   Joe Gibbs
Primary Sponsors   Interstate Batteries/MNBA
Make of Car   Pontiac Grand Prix

Evernham Motorsports
Car Number   19
Driver   Casey Atwood
Location   Harrisburg, NC
Crew Chief   TBA
Car Owner   Evernham Motorsports
Primary Sponsor   Motorola
Make of Car   Dodge Intrepid R/T

Joe Gibbs Racing Inc.
Car Number   20
Driver   Tony Stewart
Location   13415 Reese Blvd. West
                   Huntsville, NC
Crew Chief   Greg Zipadelli
Car Owner   Joe Gibbs
Primary Sponsor   The Home Depot
Make of Car   Pontiac Grand Prix

Wood Brothers Racing
Car Number   21
Driver   Elliot Sadler
Location   Stuart, VA
Crew Chief   TBA
Car Owner   Glen Wood
Primary Sponsor   Mororcraft
Make of Car   Ford Taurus

Bill Davis Racing Inc.
Car Number   22
Driver   Ward Burton
Location   301 Old Thomasville Road
                   High Point, NC
Crew Chief   Tommy Baldwin
Car Owner   Bill Davis
Primary Sponsor   Caterpillar
Make of Car   Dodge Intrepid R/T

Hendrick Motorsports
Car Number   24
Driver   Jeff Gordon
Location   4433 Papa Joe Hendrick Blvd.
                   Harrisburg, NC
Crew Chief   Robbie Loomis
Car Owner   Rick Hendrick
Primary Sponsor   DuPont Automotive Finishes
Make of Car   Chevrolet Monte Carlo

Hendrick Motorsports
Car Number   25
Driver   Jerry Nadeau
Location   4433 Papa Joe Hendrick Blvd.
                   Harrisburg, NC
Crew Chief   Tony Furr
Car Owner   Joe Hendrick Motorsports
Primary Sponsor   Michael Holigan
Make of Car   Chevrolet Monte Carlo

Haas-Carter Motorsports
Car Number   26
Driver   Jimmy Spencer
Location   2670 Peachtree Road
                   Statesville, NC
Crew Chief   Donnie Wingo
Car Owners   Carl Haas/Travis Carter
Primary Sponsor   Big Kmart
Make of Car   Ford Taurus

Eel River Racing
Car Number   27
Driver   Kenny Wallace
Location   208 Rolling Hills Road
                   Mooresville, NC
Crew Chief   Barry Dodson
Car Owner   Jack Birmingham
Primary Sponsor   TBA
Make of Car   Pontiac Grand Prix

Robert Yates Racing, Inc.
Car Number   28
Driver   Ricky Rudd
Location   292 Rolling Hills Road
                   Mooresville, NC
Crew Chief   Michael McSwain
Car Owner   Robert Yates
Primary Sponsors   Texaco/Havoline
Make of Car   Ford Taurus

Richard Childress Racing
Car Number   31
Driver   Mike Skinner
Location   236 Industrial Drive
                   Welcome, NC
Crew Chief   TBA
Car Owner   Richard Childress
Primary Sponsor
Make of Car   Chevrolet Monte Carlo

PPI Motorsports
Car Number   32
Driver   Rickey Craven
Location   3051 First Avenue Court S.E.
                   Hickory, NC
Crew Chief   Mike Beam
Car Owner   Cal Wells III
Primary Sponsor   Tide
Make of Car   Ford Taurus

Andy Petree Racing
Car Number   33
Driver   Joe Nemechek
Location   Flat Rock, NC
Crew Chief   Andy Petree
Car Owner   Andy Petree
Primary Sponsor   Oakwood Homes
Make of Car   Chevrolet Monte Carlo

MB2 Motorsports
Car Number   36
Driver   Ken Schrader
Location   185 McKenzie Road
                   Mooresville, NC
Crew Chief   Sammy Johns
Car Owners   Nelson Bowers/Tom
                   Beard/Read Morton
Primary Sponsor   M&Ms
Make of Car   Pontiac Grand Prix

Ganassi Racing
Car Number   40
Driver   Sterling Marlin
Location   114 Meadow Hill Circle
                   Mooresville, NC
Crew Chief   Scott Eggleston
Car Owner   Ganassi Motorsports
Primary Sponsor   Coors Light
Make of Car   Chevrolet Monte Carlo

Petty Enterprises
Car Number 43
Driver John Andretti
Location 311 Branson Mill Road
Randleman, NC
Crew Chief Greg Steadman
Car Owner Richard Petty
Primary Sponsors STP/Cheerios
Make of Car Dodge Intrepid R/T

Petty Enterprises
Car Number 44
Driver Buckshot Jones
Location 311 Branson Mill Road
Randleman, NC
Crew Chief Mark Tutor?
Car Owner Kyle Petty
Primary Sponsor Georgia Pacific
Make of Car Dodge Intrepid R/T

Petty Enterprises
Car Number 45
Driver Kyle Petty
Location Thomasville, NC
Crew Chief Chris Hussey
Car Owner Kyle Petty
Primary Sponsor Sprint PCS
Make of Car Dodge Intrepid R/T

Midwest Transit Racing
Car Number 50
Driver Rick Mast
Location 4909 Stough Road
Concord, NC
Crew Chief John Monsam
Car Owner Hal Hicks
Primary Sponsor Midwest Transit
Make of Car Chevrolet Monte Carlo

Andy Petree Racing
Car Number 55
Driver Bobby Hamilton
Location 1100 Upward Road
Flat Rock, NC
Crew Chief Jimmy Elledge
Car Owner Andy Petree
Primary Sponsors Square D/Cooper Lighting
Make of Car Chevrolet Monte Carlo

Haas-Carter Motorsports
Car Number 66
Driver Todd Bodine
Location 2670 Peachtree Road
Statesville, NC
Crew Chief Larry Carter
Car Owners Carl Haas/Travis Carter
Primary Sponsors Route 66/Big Kmart
Make of Car Ford Taurus

Marcis Auto Racing
Car Number 71
Driver Dave Marcis
Location 71 Beale Road
Arden, NC
Crew Chief Robert Marcis
Car Owner Helen Marcis
Primary Sponsor Realtree
Make of Car Chevrolet Monte Carlo

Galaxy Motorsports
Car Number 75
Driver Wally Dallenbach Jr.
Location 223 Rolling Hills Road
Mooresville, NC
Crew Chief Wayne Orme
Car Owner Darwin Oordt
Primary Sponsor TBA
Make of Car Ford Taurus

Jasper Motorsports
Car Number 77
Driver Robert Pressley
Location 110 Knob Hill Road
Mooresville, NC
Crew Chief Ryan Pemberton
Car Owners Doug Bawel/Mark
Wallace/Mark Harrah
Primary Sponsors Jasper Engines/Federal Mogul
Make of Car Ford Taurus

Robert Yates Racing Inc.
Car Number 88
Driver Dale Jarrett
Location 115 Dwelle Street
Charlotte, NC
Crew Chief Todd Parrott
Car Owner Robert Yates
Primary Sponsor UPS
Make of Car Ford Taurus

Melling Racing Ent.
Car Number 92
Driver Stacy Compton
Location 4366 Triple Crown Drive
Concord, NC
Crew Chief Jerry Pitts
Car Owner Mark Melling
Primary Sponsors Kodiak/Cougar
Make of Car Dodge

Bill Davis Racing
Car Number 93
Driver Dave Blaney
Location 301 Old Thomasville Road
High Point, NC
Crew Chief Gil Martin
Car Owner Bill Davis
Primary Sponsors Amoco Oil Co./Siemens
Make of Car Dodge

Roush Racing
Car Number 97
Driver Kurt Busch
Location Concord, NC
Crew Chief TBA
Car Owner Jack Roush
Primary Sponsor TBA
Make of Car Ford Taurus

Roush Racing
Car Number 99
Driver Jeff Burton
Location 122 Knob Hill Road
Mooresville, NC
Crew Chief Frank Stoddard
Car Owner Jack Roush
Primary Sponsor Citgo
Make of Car Ford Taurus

Ganassi Racing
Car Number 01
Driver TBA
Location 114 Meadow Hill Circle
Mooresville, NC
Crew Chief Tony Glover
Car Owner Ganassi Motorsports
Primary Sponsor BellSouth
Make of Car Chevrolet Monte Carlo

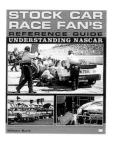

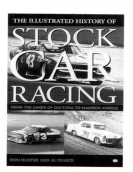

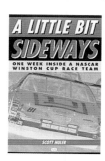